Soft Borders, Hard Edges

Bent Street 5.1 : Australian LGBTIQA+ Art, Writing & Ideas

a special edition focusing on the trans and gender diverse community

Edited by:

Sam Elkin
Yves Rees

Series Editor-in-Chief: Tiffany Jones

Clouds of Magellan Press | Melbourne

Bent Street: Australian LGBTIQA+ Arts, Writing & Ideas is published twice yearly by Clouds of Magellan Press, Melbourne. www.cloudsofmagellanpress.net

bentstreet.net

ISSN 2652-659X (Print)
ISBN: (paperback) ISBN: 978-0-6451935-1-0

Series Editor-in-Chief: Tiffany Jones
Editorial Advisor: Dennis Altman
Contributing Editors and *Bent Street* ambassadors: Ashley Sievwright, Gordon Thompson, Guy James Whitworth, Margie Fischer, Henry von Doussa.

Bent Street logo: Andrew Liu

Design: Gordon Thompson

Publication and distribution, Lightning Source, through eBook Alchemy. ebookalchemy.com

Cover image: 'Vessel' by Samuel Beatty—https://www.samuellukeart.com/

Back cover image: 'Kalypso' by Jamie James— http://jamesphoto.com.au/

Acknowledgement

Bent Street acknowledges the Traditional Custodians of country throughout Australia and their connections to land, sea and community. We pay our respect to their Elders past, present and emerging, and extend that respect to all Aboriginal and Torres Strait Islander peoples.

Contents

Introduction
TIFFANY JONES

Welcome to *Bent Street*, which now bends around the soft borders and hard edges of gender, in guest editors Sam and Yves' trans issue. They ensure our street twirls around the tongue-twisters, spoonerisms, stitchings and paint daubs of talented mixed media artists who depict the art of living – like good judy, Samuel Luke Beatty and Sav Zwickl. We wind through the writings of poets like Kait Fenwick, Adele Aria and Ruth Dahl; and spiral through the stories of trans refugees Clair and Purity as they travelled across various kinds of borders in and from Uganda to Kenya, or Kenya to Sweden.

Our road also whorls around significant contemporary thinking on trans issues fresh from the professoriate: Sociology Professor Emerita Raewyn Connell discusses the most important issues from a perspective that centres trans peoples' interests. Gender and Sexuality Studies Associate Professor Lucy Nicholas explores tensions and potentials for greater common ground across feminism, LGBT rights, trans, and queer gender interests. A team led by Psychology Professor Damien Riggs considers how men, trans/masculine and non-binary people negotiate conception against a context of social norms.

Finally, we veer onto the main drag and byways of gender diverse representation; picturing Jamie James' photography of thriving community members and collecting Reid Marginalia's gender euphoric archive armour along the way … Buckle up!

Tiffany Jones – Editor-in-Chief

Spilling the T
SAM ELKIN & YVES REES

Yves: Sam, this special issue of *Bent Street* had its origins in the Spilling the T Collective. How would you describe that project?

Sam: The Spilling the T Collective is a trans and gender diverse writers' group that we set up as part of Transgender Victoria's SPARK peer support project in early 2020. We basically set it up to foster more trans and gender diverse people to get to know each other, share their stories, provide peer-to-peer feedback and get published. We had intended for it to be an in-person workshop series at the Wheeler Centre, but due to the pandemic, we had to re-jig it to be an online workshop and guest speaker series. It kicked off in May 2020 and we had over thirty trans and gender diverse people participate from across so-called Australia. We had some really amazing guest speakers address the group along the way like the award-winning poets Ellen van Neerven and Rae White, as well as the comedian and performance artist Krishna Istha. We ran a second workshop series in late 2020 too that Marcel Liemant facilitated, who was one of our round one participants and an accomplished YA fantasy writer.

Did you enjoy being a part of the writers' group?

Yves: Yes – perhaps especially due to the online aspect. Although going digital was a COVID-induced necessity, it turned out that operating as a virtual writers' group actually enhanced the experience. It allowed us to include and connect with trans and gender diverse writers from all around the country, rather than just those living in physical proximity to the Wheeler Centre in Melbourne's CBD. We ended up with writers from Perth, Adelaide, Sydney, regional Tasmania, Brisbane, Newcastle and elsewhere. Given that trans and queer communities tend to cluster around Sydney and Melbourne, it was very meaningful to connect with trans and gender diverse folk living outside these southeast metropolitan hubs. These writers taught me a great deal about the diversity of trans experience and provided a much-needed sense of community at a time of physical isolation from queer spaces. Our pivot to digital platforms also allowed us to hear from international guest speakers – including Thomas Page McBee, a US trans memoirist, journalist and screenwriter who zoomed in from his home in California. Finally, the Spilling the T experience opened my eyes to the sheer size and enormous talent of the trans writing community. I had expected only a handful of participants and was blown away when we commenced the first round with over thirty writers.

What did Spilling the T teach you about trans writing in this country?

Sam: Almost everyone we met along the way, whether they came to every session or just a couple made a huge impression on me. Some of them were really hurting, struggling with poverty, alienating healthcare and the administrative burden of day-to-day living. Some of them had been through really hard times before, but were now living their best lives. So many of us have experienced chronic traumatization from familial and community rejection and many of those experiences really spilled out onto the page in one way or another. Despite that, no two stories were ever the same. I also think people got heaps out of reading each other's stories, as many hadn't really had access to a lot of trans and gender diverse writing before. Some participants had had a few essays or poems published in Australian literary journals before, but most had just been writing for themselves, and didn't really see a clear path to publication anywhere. It just made me feel quite motivated to do what I could to create that pathway for trans and gender diverse people. It's much less burdensome to share your own experiences when you don't have to worry that people will think that 'this is the only trans experience'. So, yeah, more than anything, I think this project taught me about the power of taking the time to invite marginalised people to come together as a group and be creative. You can see the results of giving people a deadline in this anthology! It's inspiring.

Do you feel like Spilling the T Collective impacted on your own writing in any way?

Yves: The Collective gave me a sense of being part of something bigger than my own story. The Spilling the T experience, combined with our work guest-editing this special issue of *Bent Street*, made me realise that my personal trans writing is situated within a broader cultural moment in which trans and gender diverse people are telling their own stories *en masse* for the first time. Of course, trans people are nothing new, and there's powerful trans writing dating back many decades, but I also believe (with my historian hat on here) that we're currently in the midst of something unprecedented: a mass profusion of trans storytelling that is cutting through to cis audiences and changing broader conversations about gender. We know that there's been a huge upsurge in presentations to gender clinics over the past decade and I suspect we're now seeing the cultural fruits of all these 'coming outs'. It's an exciting time. There's so much trans and gender diverse writing entering the world. In addition to this issue of *Bent Street*, this year has also seen the publication of Nevo Zisin's *The Pronoun Lowdown* and Kaya Wilson's *As Beautiful As Any Other*. S. J. Norman's short-story collection *Permafrost* will be published by UQP in October, my own memoir *All About Yves: Notes from a Transition* is due out with Allen & Unwin in August, and Bastian Fox Phelan's memoir is slated for publication with Giramondo in late 2021. Five trans-authored books in one year! This is surely unprecedented within the small Australian publishing landscape. Not to mention the glorious YA fiction of Alison Evans (whose latest work, *Euphoria Kids*, came out in 2020), the criticism and essays of people like Oliver Reeson, Jinghua Qian, Maddee Clark and Alex Gallagher, and the award-winning poetry of Ellen van Neerven (whose 2020 collection *Throat* won Book of the Year at the 2021 NSW Premier's Awards). It feels like a golden age and I can't wait to see what the next few years will bring. Of course, it's not all roses. Increased trans acceptance and visibility has also prompted an alarming transphobic backlash. But this trans writing is, slowly but surely, shifting the culture in profound ways. As Rebecca Solnit writes, 'the change that counts in revolution takes place first in the imagination'. Through telling trans stories, we can remake the world. In Solnit's words, 'stories trap us, stories free us, we live and die by stories'.

What are your hopes for the future of trans storytelling?

Sam: I want to read about funny or unlikeable trans people whose lives don't follow an inspirational narrative arc. I want to read trans characters whose gender history is not central to the plotline. I want to read stories that lift the lid on complex issues that we're reluctant to put on the page because we're worried that we'll be policed by our own community for not 'staying on message'. But more generally, I want everyone, trans or otherwise, to be able to share their stories without being limited by the increasingly restrictive global publishing industry. I think we need to bear in mind that the market forces bearing down on us to tell the 'right' trans story in order to get published are the same kinds of pressures that are bearing down on all kinds of marginalised people. I'd love to see a renaissance in publishing outside the mainstream more generally. That's why I support the work of small publishers like Subbed In, Zer0 books and Arsenal Pulp Press. Not to mention *Bent Street*!

What do you think readers are going to take from this edition of *Bent Street*, which includes authors from Spilling the T Collective and a whole bunch of others who responded to our open call out?

Yves: I suspect readers will be struck by the penetrating insight of trans subjectivity. More and more, I believe our position on the margins forces trans people to become experts in all things gender, bodies and identity. In contrast to the average cis person, trans people tend to have an acute understanding of how embodied subjects construct and perform gendered selves – an understanding that, while often borne of pain and trauma, also makes for memorable writing. We see nuances that often elude the cis gaze. That distinctive trans ability to dissect how gender works – for all people, cis and trans – is something that shines through in this edition of *Bent Street*. I also think readers may note that we trans people set high standards for ourselves. Even though just surviving this transphobic world is a remarkable act of resistance, the trans voices featured here are striving to be more, do more, understand more. To be the best possible version of our remade selves. You could say this represents internalised transphobia – the harsh inner critic always demanding more. But you could also say it is a testament to a trans commitment to living an examined life. When you've questioned something as foundational as your gender, everything else becomes subject to question as well. Perhaps questioning, searching, striving, wondering about everything is part of what it means to be trans? It certainly strikes me as a core theme in these pages.

What's your perspective on the contents of the special issue?

Sam: It's just been such a treat seeing it all come together. Collaborating with *Bent Street* gave us the opportunity to create a national anthology of writers from far beyond Naarm where we're both based. I also love seeing hugely influential thinkers like Professor

Emerita Raewyn Connell included alongside emerging trans and gender diverse writers, some of whom are first-time authors. I've always adored the eclectic nature of *Bent Street*, it's an intergenerational queer party where everyone is invited. I am really proud to be able to publish *This is my Story* by Stacey Stokes; an incarcerated trans woman, as it's too easy for us to forget that many trans women are still locked up in men's prisons across so-called Australia. A couple of the poems including Ruq's *Queer Me Crazy // Allies (All-lies?)* and Anastasia Le's *Labels* were originally written for live storytelling events that I produced for Midsumma, so it was really satisfying getting to see these moving pieces given a new life on the page.

Any final thoughts?

Yves: It's been a real pleasure to work with you and all the writers on Spilling the T and this issue of *Bent Street*. As someone who is still a 'baby trans', these collaborations have taught me so much about what it means to live outside cisnormativity. I'm damn proud of the final product, which I think captures the gamut of trans and gender diverse experience. We see that trans people are still fighting for basic rights and, in some cases, survival. The pieces here don't shy away from that stark reality. But we also see that trans and gender diverse folk are so much more than victims of a transphobic world. We're three-dimensional humans, as complicated and messy and beautiful as anyone on this planet. It's a privilege to publish the work of such a creative, radical and kind group of humans. Onwards towards trans liberation!

Sam Elkin is a trans masculine writer and radio maker living in the western suburbs of Naarm (Melbourne). Sam's essays have previously been published in the *Griffith Review*, *Overland* literary journal and *Kill Your Darlings*. In 2021, he received an Australian Society of Authors Award Mentorship program, and he is currently working on a debut essay collection.

Dr Yves Rees is a writer and historian living on Wurundjeri land. At present, they're a Lecturer in History at La Trobe University and co-host of the podcast Archive Fever. Yves' essay 'Reading the Mess Backwards' was awarded the 2020 Calibre Essay Prize and their memoir *All About Yves: Notes from a Transition* will be published by Allen& Unwin in September 2021.

I TUCKED TH
SHAVER UNDE
MY ARM AND GAV
IT A NEW HOME I
MY BATHROO
CABINET.
PLACED IT NEX
TO THE OTHE
GROOMING PARA
PHERNALIA I'
BEEN COLLECTIN
WHILE I WAS WAIT
ING FOR M
BEARD TO FIL
OUT. I HAD BEAR
OIL, SHAVIN
SOAP, SHAVIN
GEL, A SHAVIN

Turned out alright
BRON RICHARDSON

'If you want anything, take it,' Mum said, as I noticed the pile of boxes and old shopping bags by the garage door. 'It's all going to the op-shop in a few days.' Mum had been clearing out again. It was mostly Dad's old stuff. It made me sad seeing his things leave the house, but I could also see how this process was helping Mum to heal. It was all just stuff after all. Objects. His memory could never just be cleared out. Mum sorted through everything before it made it to the op-shop pile. Filtering out what should stay and what should go. Sobbing one minute as she found cards and love notes he'd kept for decades and then cursing him the next as she found receipts and bank documents that were just as old. I could see the logic in her decisions, I mean who really needs old shoe boxes full of stationary or hundreds of salvaged zip lock bags or the small Tupperware containers that Dad used to store his knick-knacks, most of which were empty? Just things, stuff. Holding sentimental value only to Dad.

I looked down and saw a bunch of old books and was reminded of how Dad would read to my brother and I when we were children. I remember him reading me Enid Blyton's *Famous Five*. A family friend once said that I reminded her of Georgina, one of the main characters, a fierce tomboy with short hair just like mine, who liked to be called George and was delighted when people mistook her for a boy. Dad would sit by our bedside and read a chapter to us each night before bed, maybe even two if we were lucky! Years later, in a painful role-reversal, I would read to Dad in bed in the weeks leading up to his death.

I sighed and turned to walk away …

As I did so, something caught my eye on top of one of the boxes. Dad's old electric shaver. Well one of them at least. True to form, Dad had several over the years and would never throw any of them away. I looked down and saw the brown faux leather case. I picked it up and opened it to reveal the red velvety vacuum formed plastic presenting the Phillipshave HP1601. Black and grey circa 1980s. Dad had kept the manual and spare rotor blades with a handwritten note recording the purchase date for future reference: Sept' 2007.

Was this the moment that I had been so desperately searching for? A sign from Dad beyond the grave to symbolise his blessing? A way in which we could share that quintessential coming-of-age moment when a father teaches his son to shave?

You see, I never came out to Dad. By the time I'd figured it all out, by the time I'd accepted that transitioning was the only way forward in my life, Dad was dying. He knew it, I knew it. Deep down I knew it didn't matter to him. One of the last things he said to me was that I 'turned out alright'. I knew he accepted me and that I would never lose his love. I chose not to tell him, not because I was scared that he might reject me, but rather to spare him the pain of knowing he'd miss seeing me grow into a happier version of myself. It was a time of saying goodbye, not hello.

Perhaps it was poor timing on my part or perhaps things turned out exactly how they were meant to be. You see, I'd known for some time that I was trans. It just took me a while to find the language to explain it. I'd always liked myself as a child and I was lucky enough to have loving parents who let me express myself through short haircuts and boyish clothes. I could walk through the world comfortably for the most part. I never gave the idea of being trans much thought, or at least I never associated myself with that word. Trans people were often portrayed so negatively on TV or in movies; they were usually the punch line of a joke or a villainous serial killer. Once their trans identity was discovered, they were either laughed at or punished. I learned through popular culture that trans people were worthy of ridicule and that the beating or killing of trans people was completely justifiable. I didn't want to be trans. The life of a trans person seems so traumatic. Why risk getting laughed at, beaten or worse?

Then I realised that the life of a trans person, the life that I was so afraid of, was the life I was already living. I wore masculine clothes every day because they hid the girly parts of my body that I hated so much. Strangers would misgender me all the time and I would often get harassed in women's bathrooms. People would laugh or insult me once my transness was revealed. I was already living as a trans person. The risk of getting laughed at, beaten or worse was with me every day. The anxiety and dysphoria would be there with me for the rest of my life regardless of whether or not I acknowledged it. I was already trans, I just didn't call myself that. Once I realised that trans was probably the best word to describe me, I figured I should just own it. So what if I was trans? I owed it to myself to be happy; I only get one life after all. After watching Dad pass away, I realised that life could end so suddenly. At least with HRT and surgery I could like my body a little better and enjoy whatever life was still ahead of me.

As the weeks and months passed after Dad's death, I began my transition legally and medically. During this time, I started to develop a new relationship with my masculinity. This was a form of masculinity that I'd never known before. A physically embodied one. It was in my veins, in my blood. I saw it in the subtle changes in my jawline and shoulders and heard it in my voice as it lowered an octave. It meant a new way of walking through the world. Things were different now. In my previous butch form, I was perceived to be either too young or too effeminate to be capable of aggression or violence. The softness of my shape and pitch of my voice allowed me to be assertive without being threatening. I could be questioned easily or simply dismissed. Even with my small frame, my new baritone and stubbly form meant people interacted with me differently. Especially with my pale skin. I was taken more seriously. Some strangers, especially women, seemed slightly intimidated by my presence. I soon realised that the world now saw me as a straight white man and all that was associated with that stereotype. My new exterior was synonymous with entitlement, misogyny and violence.

My queerness was becoming invisible. I grieved for my lost butchhood as I fell in love with my new body. I didn't want to be a straight white man, but I also didn't want to be a queer woman. I wanted to be the kind and gentle person I'd always been. I studied my behaviour and tried to adjust myself accordingly. I'd try to be a better person than that straight white man that I was presumed to be. I'd tell myself: *Do not tower over her. Allow him to be vulnerable with you. Provide space. Do not block the door. Do not mansplain. Ask questions but do not be intrusive. Do not assume. Be explicit when you ask for consent; it is not always implied. Let them speak and listen. Really listen. Be polite. Be humble. Be chivalrous but know when it's unwelcome, and never ever be chauvinistic.* If I was going to be seen as a straight white man then I had to be the best straight white man I could be. I had to navigate this new path now without the best straight white man role model that I'd ever known. My Dad. I missed his gentleness and thoughtfulness.

I tucked the shaver under my arm and gave it a new home in my bathroom cabinet. I placed it next to the other grooming

paraphernalia I'd been collecting while I was waiting for my beard to
fill out. I had beard oil, shaving soap, shaving gel, a shaving brush, a
twin blade razor, a beard trimmer and an old-fashioned stainless steel
single blade safety razor I'd bought online. I could've opened a barber
shop if I'd wanted too!

I'd been fascinated by all things barbershop since I was a child. A
sacred world of men's grooming and self-care that I wasn't privy to.
Growing up, I'd once seen k.d. lang on the cover of *Vanity Fair*
magazine. The one where she's sitting in a barber's chair getting
shaved by Cindy Crawford. She looked so blissful sitting there,
shaving cream brushed on above her Cheshire smile in the shape of a
moustache, as she let Cindy take the cutthroat razor to her face. The
image captivated me in ways that I couldn't articulate at the time. k.d.
represented a type of masculinity that was desired by women, or at
least by Cindy in that image. Her butchness was so appealing. I
wanted to be just like her. I'd play make-believe games in the secrecy
of my bedroom, pretending that I was getting ready for a date with
my imaginary girlfriend. I'd make razors out of Lego and scrape
moisturiser off my face when I was certain nobody would see me.
When I was done, I'd hide my plastic brick razor so far under my bed
an adult would struggle to climb under and find it. I intuitively knew
that this wasn't something that I was supposed to dream about.
Maybe if I hadn't had so much shame, I could have asked Dad more
about shaving and learnt from him. I wonder what he would have
said. Would he have taught me?

I closed the cabinet door and looked in the mirror at my changing
face. The soft wispy hairs on my chin had begun to turn thick and
wiry. Not quite a beard yet but it was a start. Just enough to form a
patch that could be seen from a distance. Enough to take a razor to if
I so desired. I decided to take this moment and live out my childhood
fantasy. It wasn't quite the Cindy-Crawford-barber-shop experience
or Dad-teaching-me-to-shave lesson; but still, perhaps this was a good
opportunity to change my raggedy look? Maybe a little tweak to my
appearance could help in my quest to be seen as the best straight
white man that I could be? After all, Dad was nearly always clean
shaven. Maybe a shave could make me appear a little softer around
the edges, smooth, perhaps somewhat more approachable? Besides, a
little self-care was a good place to start when it comes to being the
best version of oneself. I'd watched enough episodes of *Queer Eye* to

know that! Plus, my oddly shaped chin patch just looked weird. Time to go, my little hairy friend.

I got Dad's shaver out and plugged it in. I paused. Was there a technique to this? I wondered. Dad's voice echoed through my head, 'Read the instructions'. I rolled my eyes like a teenager. 'Yes Dad' I said to myself. Sure enough, there were instructions in the case. Dad never threw anything out. After a quick tutorial I began. Buzz. That sound. It took me right back to being a child and hearing Dad shave every morning. The noise echoing throughout the house. Did Dad shave the same way? I hope I was doing it right. 'Move shaver in a circular motion' the instructions said. I think Dad did it this way. I wish I'd paid more attention.

Then I remember the shame I felt. Shaving was not something meant for me. I tried to not be so curious about it. I shied away whenever Dad was shaving or when my brother started shaving. That's why I had to be sure nobody was watching when I had my Lego grooming sessions before imaginary date night. No, I thought. No more shame. I don't have to hide anymore. I'm allowed to do this. Buzz. My whiskers fell off my chin and landed in the sink. This moment was meant for me, I said to myself as I gave myself permission. Buzz. I shaved my cheeks, shedding myself of my beard and my shame. Buzz. Maybe Dad left the shaver behind for me for this very moment? Buzz. Maybe he just didn't like throwing things away? Buzz. Either way, I'm here right now, in this moment trying to be a better person in so many ways. I'd just have to own it, I thought. Just like I owned my transness. Buzz. I 'turned out alright.' Dad's voice in my head again. Buzz. I cleaned up my sideburn area. All done. I looked in the mirror. My face naked and exposed. Smaller and vulnerable without its manly mask but I knew it would grow back. Maybe I have 'turned out alright'. But I knew I was still turning out. I would continue to grow just as my beard did. I put Dad's shaver back in the cabinet. I only hoped that I could continue to turn out alright and be the best person I could be. I looked at my reflection again. Even if the world did see me as a straight white man.

bio next page >

Bron 'Richo' Richardson is a Naarm-based sometimes drag performer, sometimes writer and sometimes basketball player. Full time lover of pizza (especially with pineapple), puns and cheesy jokes.

Abandon | JORDIE SLONIM

That abandoned house. Weatherboard slats dropped, fallen, swayed. Foliage growth, sprouting's scattered, painting splashes of aliveness amongst dilapidation. I pass this rustic space everyday on the bus. The longing to take up residence builds. I focus the forces necessary to temporarily disintegrate my physical body. I return to stardust, to alter time and space, emerging, as sparkling dust particles, over the overgrown front yard.

Physical form begins the process of materialisation. Dust forms into skeletal system. Blood flows to form organ and organ and more organ, piling atop and aside each other. They connect. They talk. They get functions moving. Lymph system detoxifies. Sinews grow and muscle and tendon and ligament. Chakras and meridians take their place; opening, swirling. Auric fields sweep to create as the skin organ forms, taking its multilayered place in the scheme of things. Hair, nails, teeth. A process taking seconds and lifetimes. Skin on grass, soil, worm. The cracks in the weatherboards scream their invitation to join with this space.

I liquefy. I allow my form to slither towards the lowest crack, climb over rusted nail, splintered wood and termites. I pour through the gaping chasm. Physical self-reforms. It is washed clean of suppression, oppression and erasure of true self. Whole. Queer. They. Luminous. Scattered soil on floorboards, textured steps towards shafts of light beaming through higher fissures. Feet on earthed boards. Scraping, spiralling sounds. Dust flecks dance in the light play to welcome entry. Turning a corner, all beams converge onto one blob on the floor. A plant has pushed through the spaces between with a single purple flower. My form begins to dissolve, magnified towards this light patch. I am under, inside, slithering down along this vine to emerge into a vast crystalline cave. There is a knowing. I am the cave and the cave is me. I am abandoned and abandoning. I am whole and divided, rustic and shiny, light and dark. Everything and nothing. Non-duality. With that knowing, my form is sucked back through a portal, pixelated, back onto that bus. Back to smallness. Back to a school. Back into a world of surviving the suppression, the erasure. The temporary escape may just be enough. Until tomorrow, passing this space, I begin again.

Jordie is a 48-year-old queer and gender queer human who is currently writing a memoir. Their lifelong exploration of the corporeal in relation to the spiritual informs their writing style. Jordie grew up as a dancer and choreographer, and now works as a kinesiologist and kinesiology teacher.

Thrive
JAMIE JAMES

image: Jamie James

Jamie James photographed participants in a trans and gender diverse day of photography to build positive experiences and connection for our trans and gender diverse communities, in partnership with ACON and Trans Pride Australia. Jamie project managed and headed the team behind the cameras, which also included photographers Andrea Francolini and Lexy Potts. From 70 portraits, 8 have been selected for inclusion in *bent street*.

On the facing page, Shae answers the question, 'what keeps you thriving'.

Seven more images from this sequence appear on pp. 51, 76, 91, 111, 129, 154, 179

Jamie James' bio appears on p. 180

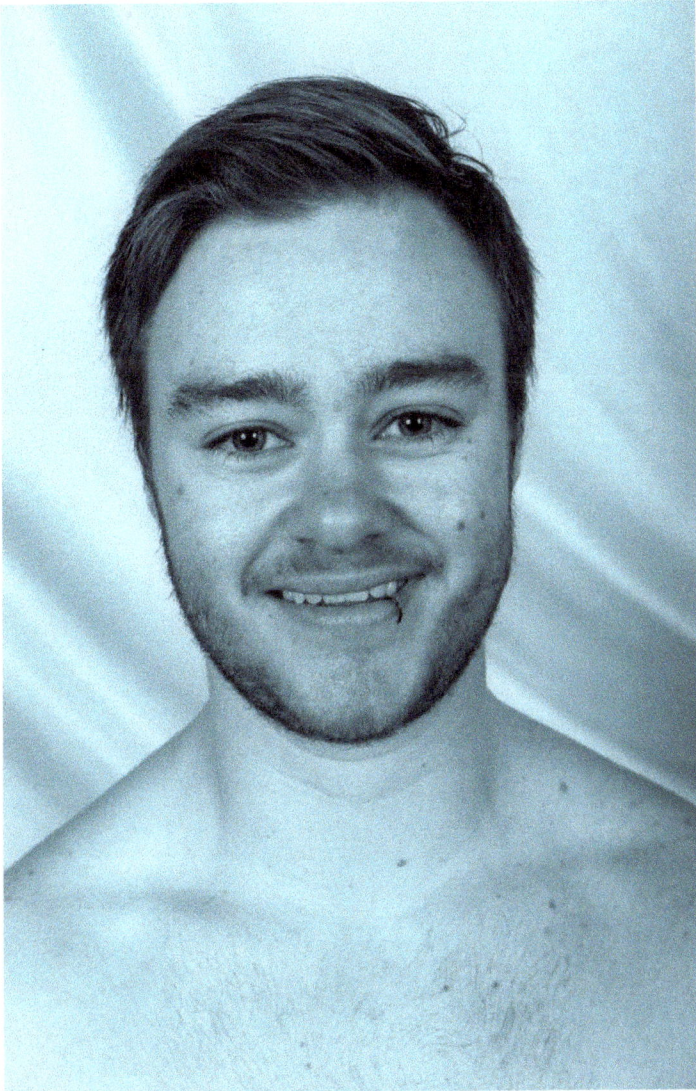

image: Jamie James

Shae

he him

I thrive by feeling connected to others and continually challenging myself to learn new things …

Yūgen*
KAIT FENWICK

*Plonking my flat, white arse on a heated seat after a 10 hour flight
across the Pacific*

Thrilled by the sound of birds singing

A Shirt worn by man in customs line reads *double poetry*,
which I've since come to learn is simply a Zara basic
absolved of any entendre

I have always been fond of the transformative sayings on the
covers of Japanese notebooks ~

My favourite:

*'I believe in friendship and the bonding connection of
human. If you are rice, the side dishes are friends. There are
likes and dislikes, but all will become energy.'*

The West is 20 years behind

Everyone is so polite, but not really

One beige Ralph Lauren clad lad announced to his mate
whilst adjusting his Calvins, in the immigration line,
'Bought a spare pair!' and his mate retorted,

'Did you plan on shitting yourself?'

I embarrass myself sneezing, waiting for the baggage on the
carousel.
To order anything is to line up, point and pray
We only get what we will settle for
The coffee machine whistles in time to Oasis's, *Fade Away*

Kinda like sitting in a bar with a gin looking up at a lambent sign that reads, *'It's good to unwind once in a while, we wish you all the luck.'*

* (幽玄): subtly profound grace, not obvious;. Datsuzoku (脱 俗): unbounded by convention, free;. Seijaku (静寂): tranquility, silence.

***

Newcastle Harbour is currently dusted pink &

I am fetishsing holding your hand through neon valleys

Of making sure your fingers jigzag with mine across lush paddyfields

Of ensuring our chapped lips brush looking over a horizon of creme terraces dotted with geraniums

I am a scramble crossing

As if you had stood there before you guided me through
Shinjuku gōruden-gai lined with
mini bars and frustrated attendants opening
and closing garage doors
and love hotels adorned with bootleg Balinese statues
holding signs reading 100,00¥/90 minutes

Of vending machines
dispensing condoms,
single serve sachets of lube

~~Sometimes~~ In certain places and spaces we are fearful of
what it means to wander hand in hand along Meiji Dori in a
way that feels different but much the same as Maitland
Road, Islington
Of what it means to occupy so much space, to be niji in a sea
of grey, amongst bodies that blend into yours but reject mine

Sensory memory echoes

fearful of not experiencing it at all

even in May our house catches draughts

riddled with dust bunnies

that no Dyson

can contain

Kait Fenwick is a transgender writer, speaker and equity and inclusion professional living on Awabakal Country. Their work has appeared in *Seen & Heard* zine, *Butch is Not a Dirty Word*, *Cordite Poetry Review*, *Archer* magazine and on the walls at China Heights Gallery, Surry Hills. In 2018, Kait published their first poetry chapbook, *Burning Between* with Puncher & Wattmann.

Skin Canvas
SAV ZWICKL

Sav Zwickl is currently completing a PhD in Gender, Sexuality and Diversity Studies at La Trobe University. They are also a researcher with the Trans Health Research Group at The University of Melbourne. Sav enjoys listening to true-crime podcasts, weekend brunch dates and road trips.

Skin canvas.

And then it is done.
Smeared across my torso,
seeping into my skin,
and bonding with my blood

Days turn into weeks
that turn into months.

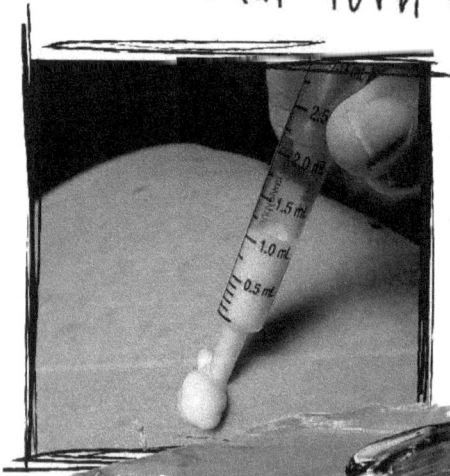

Light fluff accumulates
along my jaw line,
created by the lightest
stroke of the paint brush.

A few darker and thicker hairs start to appear a slightly darker shade of paint, made with a slightly heavier hand.

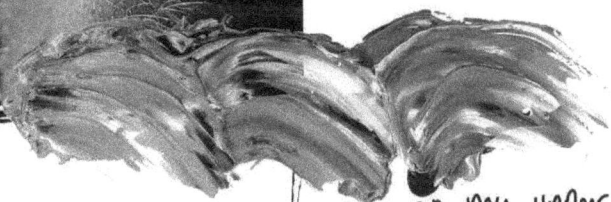

on my upper lip

around my belly button

Spreading slowly down my thighs

hundreds upon hundreds of tiny delicate brush strokes

on a skin canvas

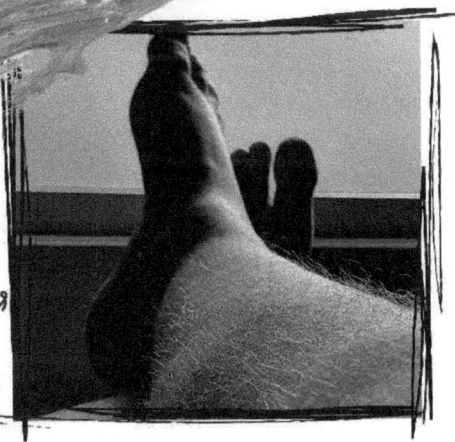

Trans Conception

Damien W. Riggs, Carla A. Pfeffer, Ruth Pearce, Sally Hines, and Francis Ray White

Men, trans/masculine and non-binary people negotiating conception: Creating new possibilities and resisting entrenched social norms.

Across the world, growing numbers of people who are not women are undertaking pregnancies. In Australia, for example, Medicare data records that on average 50 men give birth each year (Medicare, 2020). Our international study of 51 men, trans/masculine, and non-binary people explores the diverse pathways that people take to conception (Riggs et al., 2021), the potential challenges and benefits associated with each pathway, and how our participants grappled with and resisted entrenched social norms about reproduction. We briefly summarise some of our findings below.

In terms of conception, some of our participants sought out friends or acquaintances who were willing to donate sperm. For some of these participants, negotiating donor sperm through informal arrangements was a straightforward process. For these participants, donors were often seen as extended family members: as fathers to children, or as uncles. Participants often spoke about informal donor conception using humorous language, depicting friendly and caring negotiations about a complex and potentially sensitive topic.

Other participants also accessed donor sperm through informal channels, though with third parties previously unknown to them. For these participants the negotiations were somewhat more challenging. Some participants learned that donors wanted to help them conceive via intercourse, which was not appealing to our participants. Others were concerned about 'putting themselves out there' on websites designed to match donors with recipients, and were concerned about how potential donors might view them.

Yet other participants conceived via intercourse with an intimate partner. For these participants conception was arguably the most straightforward, however not without its challenges. Challenges included the timing of conception, the views of intimate partners about becoming a parent, and for a small number participants, the experience of conception as a result of non-consensual sex within a relationship.

Finally, some participants negotiated the receipt of donor sperm through a fertility clinic. For many of these participants, there were challenges associated with the cost of treatment, the attitudes and knowledge of clinic staff, and the clinical nature of fertility services. Experiences with fertility clinics was highly variable across countries, reflecting differences between countries with social health care and those without, and reflecting the willingness of clinics in different countries to provide care to men, trans/masculine and non-binary people seeking to conceive.

Despite these diverse experiences of conception, what unified our participants was two things. First, they often sought to resist entrenched social norms in regard to conception. Some participants resisted the idea that a donor should be chosen who 'matches' the characteristics of the recipient (and their partner, where relevant). Other participants resisted the idea that conception only occurs via heterosexual intercourse. And finally, some participants resisted the assumption that conception is inherently difficult for trans/masculine and non-binary people.

In addition to resistance, our participants also spoke about making pragmatic decisions when negotiating with entrenched social norms. For some participants this involved side-stepping clinic bureaucracy when trying to find a known donor. Others framed conception for men, trans/masculine, and non-binary people as not being exceptional. Finally, some participants reported undertaking cost-benefit analyses when seeking to access donor sperm through clinics.

Our findings suggest that fertility clinics have an important role to play in the normalization of conception for men, trans/masculine, and non-binary people, but that this requires education for clinic staff. However, it should not be the task of men, trans/masculine, and non-binary people to educate clinic staff. Rather, education (including ongoing professional development) is the work of fertility specialists, and this education should include training in regard to best practice for supporting men, trans/masculine, and non-binary people.

Our findings also suggest the importance of legal mechanisms to protect men, trans/masculine, and non-binary gestational parents. As the recent case of Freddie McConnell in the United Kingdom highlighted, legal determinations about men, trans/masculine, and non-binary gestational parents can significantly undermine their reproductive rights by failing to acknowledge their status as parents (for McConnell, with the Court determining that in law he should be recognised as a mother, not a father). This highlights the importance of education to ensure that Courts recognise the dignity of men, trans/masculine, and non-binary people and their right to self-determination.

In sum, as there is growing public awareness of the reproductive experiences of men, trans/masculine and non-binary people, so comes with this the need for accurate information about potential reproductive pathways. Rather than perpetuating hyperbole about 'pregnant men', what is needed are careful conversations that recognise the reproductive rights of men, trans/masculine and non-binary people, and which create spaces in which the reproductive needs of this diverse group of people can be recognized and addressed.

References

Medicare (2020). Medicare item 16519 processed from July 2013 to June 2020. Retrieved April 12, 2021, from http://medicarestatistics.humanservices.gov.au/statistics/do.jsp?_PROGRAM=/statistics/mbs_item_age_gender_report&VAR=services&STAT=count&PTYPE=finyear&START_DT=201307&END_DT=202006&RPT_FMT=by+state&GROUP=16519

Riggs, D.W., Pfeffer, C.A, Pearce, R., Hines, S., Ray White, F. (2021). Men, trans/masculine, and non-binary people negotiating conception: Normative resistance and inventive pragmatism. *International Journal of Transgender Health, 22,* 6-17.

Damien W. Riggs is a professor in psychology at Flinders University and an Australian Research Council Future Fellow. He is the author of over 200 publications on gender, family, and mental health, including (with Shoshana Rosenberg, Heather Fraser, and Nik Taylor) *Queer entanglements: Gender, sexuality and animal companionship* (Cambridge University Press, 2021).

Carla Pfeffer is an associate professor in the department of sociology at the University of South Carolina. She is the author of *Queering families: The postmodern partnerships of cisgender women and transgender men* (Oxford University Press, 2016).

Ruth Pearce is an adjunct research associate in the School of Sociology and Social Policy at the University of Leeds and the research coordinator for the Trans Learning Partnership. She is the author of *Understanding trans health: Discourse, power and possibilities* (Policy Press, 2018), and the co-editor of the collection *TERF Wars: Feminism and the fight for transgender futures* (Sage, 2020).

Sally Hines is a professor in the department of sociological studies at the University of Sheffield. She is the author of *Transforming gender: Transgender practices of identity, intimacy and care* (Routledge, 2007) and *Is gender fluid? A primer for the 21st century* (Thames and Hudson, 2018).

Francis Ray White is a senior lecturer in social science at the University of Westminster. Their research, writing and teaching is in the area of gender studies, particularly around questions of queer, trans and fat embodiment.

RUTH DAHL

Plumb Drop

Don't bury me as the first
Meihua blooms [but]
Prop me up [and]
Let me watch tears
Fall from a crook'd eye;
Caustically ingenuine [to]
Salt the earth for
A generation

Slippery Fish

Touch, and you will feel; Quivering
like the skin of a fish
nascent under your fingers

Or stretched like rope; rubber;
plastic pulled taut in dialectic
tension.

A glut of sensation all heat and
brimstone (and underneath)

Throbbing, tremor and vibration
held by the sharp angle of
my neck.

Let black suffuse the red

Boundaries

I am falling into the rhythms of domestic
life some wild thing,
dragged in and sat at the table,
taught to speak with my hands
where my voice
falters

When I focus my intentions to let my
bodily awareness slip; for a
moment I can feel the deep rumbling,
tumbling of disruption under the earth
broadcast all the tension of my body

You drag lust out of me by the point of a
fish-hook and without the satisfaction of
blood I am left
gasping for air in anticipation of my
own dissection

Artist, writer, musician, muse; Ruth Dahl is a Queer, Disabled resident of Naarm
living on stolen land.

Vessel
SAMUEL LUKE BEATTY

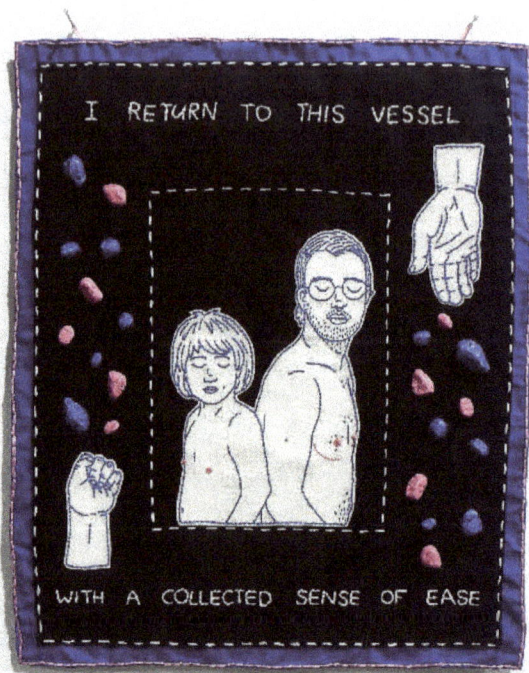

Cotton Thread, Air-Dry Clay, Embroidered on Cotton. 31cm x 37cm

'Vessel' [previous page and cover of bent street 5.1] is a hand embroidered comic about reconnecting with my childhood self and feeling at home in my body again after having top surgery. An embroidered illustration of my childhood self stands back-to-back with my current self, as I reflect, and collect memories from my childhood. I carry these memories with me, but I also let some of them go, as I continue to grow. My flat chest has returned to me, and I have a similar sense of ease of being in my body again, like I did when I was a child.

This work is embroidered on calico, using black cotton fabric as a background, with hand dyed blue cotton fabric borders. It features handmade 'rocks' made from air-dry clay and painted with pink and blue acrylic paint, sewn onto the fabric like beads. There are 11 rocks on each side to represent age 11 being the last time I had a naturally flat chest, and 11 was the date I had top surgery (11 September) and started testosterone too (11 April).

Samuel Luke Beatty is an artist who works with traditional and digital illustration, as well as forms of printmaking and bookbinding zines and artist books. His practice currently uses storytelling and the metaphor of space exploration across graphic narratives to discuss complexities of gender identity in relation to his own experiences as a transgender man. Samuel currently lives and works in Sydney, Australia.

TAZZ HISLOP

Love Comes To Town

SCORE 0069

by Taryn-Michelle Hislop

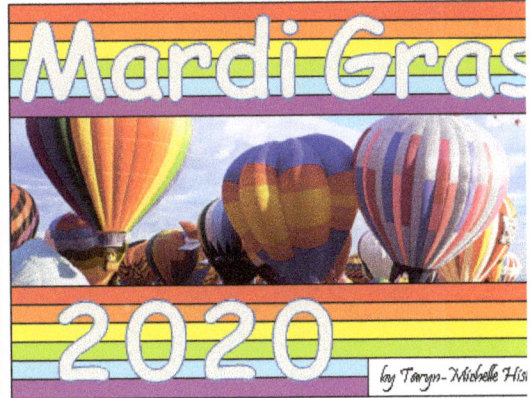

Tazz Hislop strongly supports the rights of incarcerated LGBTIQ+ individuals through the use of comics, artwork, poetry and sharing resources. Tazz's comics have previously been published in the quarterly newsletter of Inside Out Australia; an Australia-wide grassroots group supporting LGBTIQ+ people who have experienced incarceration. Tazz is currently studying for a Business degree, and loves gaming and catching up with friends and family.

ADELE ARIA

Yours or other

Born in your terms:

A witch or a warlock

Letters of spectrum
Homogenised
departure
too many hate
as if seeing
is costly
a trouble.
Intolerable ask.
Be perused and used
comfort your wrangling
permit your concept
of digestible difference
For our existence
Must be
consumable
snackable
biteable
strikable
Invisible
usable
disposable.

Your rejection
is ours.

Your comfort
holds only
minor gaps.

Navigate tomorrow
Exist today
curtain our struggle.

I can only be read,
If only you let me be.

Not a girl to be picked on

Lurching 'round shelves,
perusing with grunts
Potential customer,
heaving chest,
radiating aggression,
pauses to tumble items
in giant hands.

Seeks my smile

We play retail charade.

Interminably slow,
He finally decides

He bids
I refuse
He growls
and declares
'I thought You People
love a good bargain'

Object is thrown
I flinch inside and out

I wonder
does he read a blur of
race
and a shape of
femininity
to be so brave.

Things left unsaid

Questions resist
assumptions made fist
landmine-filled void
Humanity missed

Lines neatly drawn
Societal pawn
Cues to be read
Fight, flee and fawn

Risk being seen
Existing between
Your history
Mine named unclean

Adele Aria writes non-fiction and poetry with occasional forays in short fiction. A human rights writer-activist, they draw on studies and lived experiences of trauma, violence, disability, and queerness to explore the politics of existence and identity. They have been published in international and Australian literary and academic publications. A bi/pan+ genderqueer person of colour, Adele is grateful to be living and writing upon Noonga Boodjar.

Trans Health – Thinking Globally
RAEWYN CONNELL

I've had the good fortune to meet trans activists and support groups
in twelve countries, seven of them postcolonial countries, ranging
from rich to poor. Our conversations went across many issues, but
often came back to health. So when I was asked to write for a
research journal's special issue on 'transgender and gender diverse'
people, these talks came strongly to mind.

The special issue is here:
https://www.tandfonline.com/toc/rhsr20/current.

and my piece here:
https://www.tandfonline.com/doi/full/10.1080/14461242.2020.186
8899.
If anyone would like to read it, but can't access the text, please write to
me at raewyn.connell@sydney.edu.au and I can let you have a copy.

The majority of people who might be classified as 'trans and gender
diverse' live in postcolonial countries. Once we recognize that, trans
health discussions have to expand a long way beyond a clinical-services
model. Here's my rough-as-bags classification of the biggest issues.

1. Staying alive

I once spent an hour or two in a coffee shack in Costa Rica (yes, the
coffee is great!) with a group of *mujeres transexuales*, talking about our
lives. Somehow the talk got around to how long we expected our lives
to be. The group discussed it for a while and concluded that on
average, they expected to reach about 32. But in a neighbouring
country, where right-wing death squads were at work, it would be less.

'Social cleansing' (as the work of death squads is called), or getting
rid of sex workers, or femicide: take your pick. Many trans groups live
and work in an environment of violence, and violence can arrive for
more than one reason. Probably injury is more common than death,
but merely being bashed up can have serious consequences – being
unable to work, and being left with continuing fear.

2. Dealing with poverty

Absolute poverty exists on a much larger scale than we usually see in Australia, though heaven knows it's bad enough here. In the famous report of the WHO Commission on the Social Determinants of Health, social class inequality is the big one, operating on a global scale. Environments where socially marginalized groups live are likely to have high levels of pollution, high rates of infectious disease (TB, AIDS, COVID19), many accidents, worse food security... it adds up.

Your life may start in poverty, of course. You can also arrive in poverty through transition – being thrown out of your family, thrown out of your school, or thrown out of your factory job when transition becomes visible. If you don't have a regular income you can't afford professional reassignment surgery. You probably have to rely on hormones bought in the street. You may rely on injections of industrial silicone by an informal practitioner (I've seen a video of this work: it's skilful, but not sterile). And if you don't have money, you are in a housing crisis. That's a huge issue, where many problems come together.

3. Dealing with pressures

Trans women are not abject and not passive. Transition itself is a tremendous undertaking. There are some occupational niches that make earning a living possible. These vary locally, and from country to country. They can include hairdressing, dressmaking and theatre, and in South Asia, ritual performances at temples or weddings. The most widespread solution is sex work. The clients generally prefer young bodies, but that may not be such a big drawback if you don't expect to live long beyond your twenties.

The pressures are also political. Both evangelical and Catholic churches have become more hostile in the last ten or fifteen years. Right-wing politicians such as Orban in Hungary, Trump in the USA and Bolsonaro in Brasil have jumped aboard this campaign. (Remember the trashing of 'Safe Schools', and Morrison abusing 'gender whisperers'?) Finding allies to deal with these pressures is vital.

4. Making transitions work

Stories collected by trans groups (there's a great collection from South Africa) show the importance that families – including the ancestors – can have as resources. Making gender transitions in the long run means negotiating with authorities, including police, health and education officials, and legal systems. The more that negotiating can be done collectively, the better.

In some cases these efforts take more permanent form. In Bogotá I visited a centre, established in a dangerous area that was the centre of the sex trade, that provided *travestis* and *transexuales* with meeting rooms, health services, art facilities and certificate courses for jobs like hairdressing. It is very impressive.

There is energy and activism in trans groups around the world. Huge problems remain. I don't think the professional model of health care is capable of meeting these issues on a world scale. For that, we need a public health approach prioritising social justice. Come to think of it, that's what Australia most needs, too.

Raewyn Connell is a Professor Emerita at the University of Sydney and a Life Member of the National Tertiary Education Union. Raewyn is a transsexual woman who made a formal transition later in life. Her writing on transsexuality and other issues can be found at her blog: http://www.raewynconnell.net/

Raewyn Connell. Image: Katje Ford, courtesy Sydney Ethics Centre

Bluebottles
BROOKE MURRAY

A beach. Perhaps wind, or seagulls, or crashing waves are heard. SAMMY, early twenties, stands downstage. SAMMY is dressed casually, barefoot, hands in pockets.

SAMMY:

Mine was the shape of water. Water can bend and flow and fill containers. Water can slip through your hands and slide down drains. Disappear into vapour. Harden and freeze. No matter how water moves or transforms or is, the same chemical DNA remains. It remains the same at its very wet heart. Still something. Still present.

Sands shift as winds move them. Waves lap. The hot sun has baked the top layer of the sand so it's hard, and cracks when you walk on it. I'm watching how the sunlight kisses the water, and dances on the sea. I don't know much about light or how it works. I'd like to know more.

Kara's here. On the beach with me. The one that I come to with my family. The one that has a lagoon and rock pools. I'm afraid of slipping and falling off into the sea but Kara dances on the tips of the jagged rocks and they don't even cut her feet. Kara doesn't have any scars.

Last weekend, strong winds brought bluebottles up onto the shore. Strong winds? Or is it strong currents? I can't remember. Bluebottles show up a couple of times a year, I think. Sometimes on different beaches, sometimes on all of them.

When Kara speaks to me, her words wash over me like waves. The waves that don't break and look peaceful on the surface. When I was seven, I was the only fat kid at Nippers. It'll make you safer, said Mum. I gave up pretty quickly but not before I learnt that those waves that don't break, and look peaceful, those are the ones you have to look out for. That's how you know there's a rip that will drag you under.

We drove out here after lunch. Mum was out in the yard and Maisy had taken the dog for a walk. It was Kara's idea, actually. Can't swim after lunch, I said. We'll sink. Kara says, I don't want to swim, and she winks at me. My ears turn red and I give her a huge grin. It's not even dark yet.

We've been driving out to the beach almost every night to be alone. After dinner, this is our place. Kara's old 90s Camry hums and weaves through my sleepy hometown, taking the turn-off almost hidden completely by scrub. Each night we pull up to the lookout and open the back of the station wagon. We sit, gazing at the sunset, or at the dark ocean and its backdrop of stars. We talk, and mess around, and hold each other. Sometimes we argue. On the best nights, I fall asleep against Kara's chest, softly comforted by her deep breaths.

This time when we pull up, I follow Kara down to the beach. She's walking fast, not looking behind her. I struggle to keep up, dodging the bluebottles spread out across the shore. I'm scared of getting stung. Then, Kara stops. Sammy, she says softly, something's been going on with you since we've been here. I don't know where to look, so I watch the ocean and the sun shimmering together. That's when I begin to wonder what makes sunlight.

I should have known this was coming. I do act differently at home, around Mum, but that's not it. It's something else. Something that's harder to say. I want to tell Kara that it's nothing and let it go but I can't hide from her. The sea is in my lungs. Seaweed twirls around my legs. I'm afraid of sharks.

I have to tell her. I'm not. I don't … I dig my toes into the sand. I don't think I'm a woman, I say. I can't read my girlfriend's face.

I still love you, I whisper. I'm scared it's not enough and she's going to dump me. When you get dumped by a wave it swirls you around and around like a washing machine. Sand gets in your ears and up your nose. You could be so close to the shore and feel like you're gonna die.

Kara is watching me hold my breath. I'm waiting for her answer but she doesn't speak. Hot sun burns the back of my neck. I want her to say something. Anything. I breathe out and salty water spews out of my lungs, stinging my throat and leaving my mouth dry. Then I say the thing I don't want to say. The scary thing. The thing I won't even say to myself. I … I suppose I'm not a lesbian then.

The sand heats up under me, turning to glass and scorching my feet. The bluebottles all squirm to get away. Some of them burn. I can see downwards, through the molten sand, in a spiral towards the centre of the Earth. The skin is going to melt off my feet. Then her words come.

Sammy, I'm not a lesbian then either, if you're not a woman. I can feel the sand shifting and cooling. Kara whispers like the wind. I can't be a lesbian, she says, not if I love you. The sand cools and cools and hardens into glass. But it's still the same thing at its core, right? Silicon something …? There is so much I don't know.

Now, there is just a long glass platform stretching to the horizon. And us, little compared to everything. Don't you want to be a lesbian though? I ask and Kara smiles and shakes her head. Tears roll down my cheeks and saltwater pools at our feet.

Together we climb down the glass stairs and wade into the cool water. The sea is kind and doesn't try to kill us. When the water is up to our waists, we start to swim.

We've been swimming ever since.

Brooke Murray is a theatre maker, video artist and inclusion artist living on Wurundjeri land. In 2019, they were selected for the First Stage emerging playwrights program, supported by Melbourne Theatre Company and the Emerging Writers Festival. A reading of their short play, *Chariot*, was performed at MTC. Brooke attended the 2018 ATYP National Studio, and in 2019, their short play, *Pink Soap* was performed as part of ATYP's 'Intersection: Arrival' and published by Currency Press. Brooke took part in Antipodes Theatre Company's 2020 Winter Development Retreat where they worked with other artists to develop a piece of children's theatre called *The Moon, The Sea, You and Me*.

Transcend
LUCY NICHOLAS

Feminism, LGBT rights, trans, and queer genders: beyond the binaries and beyond the conflicts please

There are a few common critiques of gender diversity and the proliferation of gender identities (like non-binary, genderqueer etc.). Many people, including members of the LGBT+ community, argue that it puts more focus on gender as a *thing* when we actually want to get rid of it. This is often couched in the idea that we should just be 'gender blind.' On the more overtly hostile end, there are those, often from philosophy backgrounds unrelated to gender studies or from trans-exclusionary radical feminist (TERF) perspectives, who argue both binary and other trans* genders are a threat to feminism. For them, a focus on gender not ('biological') sex, and the desire to change gender itself up, undermines the reality that we live in a binary sexed world where women are subordinated in the gender order. As both an empirical sociologist (I go out and ask people things) and a social theorist (I sit and think about how things work), and a genderqueer person (I don't like binary gender), in recent work I have argued against these with some key points:

Gender-blindness is not a thing, we have a compulsory gendered world

It is well established that claims of race-blindness ('oh I don't see colour I just see people') are just code for not challenging the neutrality of whiteness and of unrecognised systemic privilege (Dagistanli 2018). A gender-blind perspective came up as a small but vocal perspective in a recent survey and focus group, conducted by myself and others on cisgender staff's attitudes to trans and gender diversity (Nicholas, Robinson & Townley 2021). The idea was that we shouldn't need special policies on, or to talk about, a person's gender identity if we treat all people the same. But we don't. Eyerolling and mockery is rarely the response to those who talk about or insist on their (cis)binary gender.

And that's because we have the 'gender rules', social norms that mean people are only intelligible within binary gender categories and its rules (Gilbert 2009). These rules are that there are two static and unchangeable genders that are naturally derived directly from the sex assigned at birth (M/F) (Bornstein 1994). And that masculinity and manhood is valued over femininity (Nicholas & Agius 2018). However, there is now almost total agreement among feminist theorists and biologists that 'biological' sex is often more fluid, non-binary and changeable than social ideas of gender. A cover of the world's leading science journal, *Nature*, even claimed that while 'biologists may have been building a more nuanced view of sex … society has yet to catch up' (Ainsworth 2015).

The 'cultural resources' of expanded genders are necessary

So, given this context, while we work on diminishing the salience of gender categories for social life, I have elsewhere argued (with Clark in Nicholas & Clark 2020) that 'despite their limits, gender 'proliferations' like nonbinary and genderqueer are the most effective and pragmatic approaches to overcoming or dismantling the gender binary whilst also expanding the range of 'cultural resources' of gender in the meantime.'

Extensive empirical studies show that, beyond access to gender affirmative medical and health care, a key need of trans and gender diverse people is on the everyday level of how people interact with us/them. Using pronouns that don't misgender or indeed gender them when they don't feel gendered, having ways to make people feel like a valid human rather than an aberration. However, for this to happen in the fundamentally gendered world we *still* live in, people need what I have elsewhere called 'cultural resources' to be able to have a framework to make sense of themselves and others in ways that don't slip back into the binaries that are so naturalised. In a massive Australian study, young trans and gender diverse 'participants valued the use of specific language and pronouns, and that could be facilitated simply by another person asking instead of assuming' (Hill et al. 2021: 146). As a start, then, beyond 'treating people how *we* would like to be treated', another way of thinking about this is that 'we should treat others how *they* would like to be treated'. And this includes with whatever gender or sexual identity, name or pronoun they would like you to use.

We need to work together on the real enemy: misogyny

Given that anybody who is not totally cisgender and / or heteronormative is breaking the gender rules they will at some point probably be policed on this. This may be in the form of women being assaulted for undermining the cultural dominance of masculinity, gay men being assaulted for being effeminate or for challenging masculinity, trans people being misgendered, or androgynous people being mocked or assaulted for breaking the binary gender rules. But these are all the result of the same underlying cause. Yale philosopher Robin Dembroff argues that this all stems from misogyny:

> Misogyny's reach extends beyond trans and non-trans women. Violence against nonbinary persons and trans men, discrimination against gay and gender-nonconforming non-trans men, and cosmetic genital surgeries on infants who are intersex are neither separate nor separable from the violence, discrimination and body policing that non-trans women constantly experience … They all are manifestations of misogyny – the force that 'patrols' and 'polices' the patriarchal order (Dembroff 2019).

I have written elsewhere that feminism is capable of being, and long has been, able to argue that both 'sex' and gender are social ideas whilst also arguing that it is so pervasive that we need to work within it, for now, to move towards getting beyond it (Nicholas 2021). As Ynda Jas says in a special issue of the *Journal of Sexual Ethics and Politics* (2020: 87), 'specificity can create visibility for alternative ways of being, which is perhaps the first step to (positively) normalising variety and diversity, while queer or similar terms perhaps have a place as the 'it doesn't matter', 'be what you want to be' ideal." I call myself a utopian realist, and I long for a feminism of both / and please!

References

Ainsworth, C (2015) 'Sex Redefined', Nature, 18th Feb 2018.

Dagistanli, S. (2018) 'When it comes to race and justice, 'colour-blindness' is not good enough' The Conversation, https://theconversation.com/when-it-comes-to-race-and-justice-colour-blindness-is-not-good-enough-106250

Dembroff, R. (2019) 'Trans women are victims of misogyny, too – and all feminists must recognize this', The Guardian https://www.theguardian.com/commentisfree/2019/may/19/valerie-jackson-trans-women-misogyny-feminism

Gilbert, M.A. (2009) 'Defeating Bigenderism: Changing Gender Assumptions in the Twenty-First Century' Hypatia 24(3): 93-112.

Hill AO, Lyons A, Jones J, McGowan I, Carman M, Parsons M, Power J, Bourne A (2021) Writing Themselves In 4: The health and wellbeing of LGBTQA+ young people in Australia. National report, monograph series number 124. Melbourne: Australian Research Centre in Sex, Health and Society, La Trobe University.

Jas, Y. (2020) 'Sexuality in a non-binary world: redefining and expanding the linguistic repertoire' Journal of Sexual Ethics and Politics, 5(1): 71-92.

Nicholas, L. (2021) 'Remembering Simone de Beauvoir's 'ethics of ambiguity' to challenge contemporary divides: Feminism beyond both sex and gender' Feminist Theory 22(2).

Nicholas, Lucy and Sal Clark (2020) 'Leave those kids alone: On the uses and abuses and feminist queer potential of non-binary and genderqueer' Journal of Sexual Ethics and Politics, 5(1).

Nicholas, Robinson and Townley (2021), Cisgender Staffs' Attitudes to and Experiences of Transgender and Gender Diversity. Western Sydney University.

Nicholas, L. & Agius, C. (2018) The Persistence of Global Masculinism. Palgrave Macmillan.

Special Issue (2020) 'Positive non-binary and / or genderqueer sexual ethics and politics' Journal of Sexual Ethics and Politics https://www.budrich-journals.de/index.php/insep/issue/view/2731 (free, open access)

Dr Lucy Nicholas – Associate Dean, International, Dean's Unit, School of Social Sciences & Associate Professor in Gender and Sexuality Studies, Anthropology & Sociology at Western Sydney University, says – 'My research specialises in gender and sexual diversities, social and political theory, queer theory, whiteness and feminisms. My first book, *Queer Post-Gender Ethics*, was published in 2014 by Palgrave McMillan and my second book, *The Persistence of Global Masculinisms*, co-authored with Chris Agius, was published in 2018. My PhD was awarded at University of Edinburgh where I worked before moving to University of Portsmouth and then to Australia. I have taught across sociology, social and political theory, gender and sexualities and academic skills and I was awarded an Australian Office of Learning and Teaching Citation for Outstanding Contributions to Student Learning in 2015'.

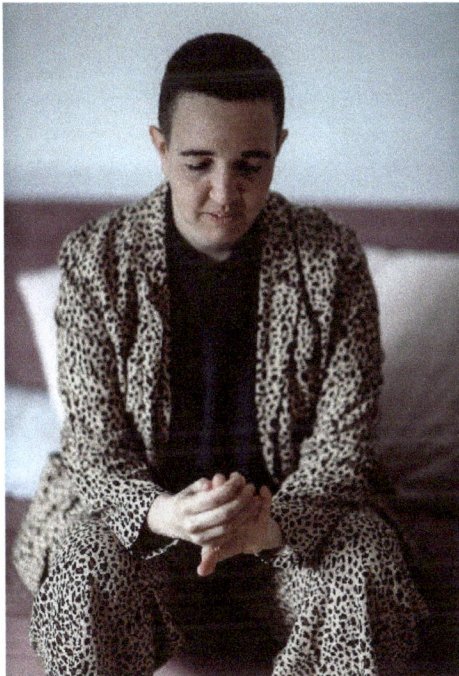

From Kakuma
CLAIR BRIANZ

Africa is a long way away from Australia. While the latest news from Uganda features the passing of new anti-gay laws, our news media is less likely to report on the plight of LGBTQIA+ refugees who arrive in Kenya from across Africa. Here are two trans women from our rainbow family whose stories deserve our attention. They represent many others whose voices are rarely heard.

'Am proud of being a Woman'

My name is Clair Brianz and I live in Kakuma refugee camp, Kenya. I am Ugandan. I got disowned by my parents once they realised that I am a girl, yet they gave birth to a boy, and they started calling me an abnormal person. Then they chased me from home and I started my own journey of life.

Now I have been living in Kakuma refugee camp for almost two years, but life has not been easy for me. I have been a target of attacks several times. I tend to always stay inside my shelter and hide because of the fear of what I have to lose. Friends have lost their lives, including a little kid who died in a scary way. I have been attacked several times, teargassed, beaten, threatened. I can't forget those moments. I am still alive and strong, but nothing has changed for the better, and I am still in pain.

Being a transgender is not an easy thing because no one can understand how I feel. Often someone might look at me and start to call me names: the devil, Satan, etc. But I hear all that and I just let it go, because no one can change my feelings and thoughts. What I do is to simply continue with my life. But however much I try, it's still very hard. I am a transgender (LGBTI) Diehard/Activist/Spirit.

THERE IS NO GOING BACK DOWN.

Over the last twelve months, it's been hard to beg and ask for help. Success largely depends on what kind of help you need and who you are asking for help. Not everyone will trust you, or help you. Those with mercy in their hearts help, so I get some little help.

For sure I am a person of peace and I want to be in better country, where I can be free, with my rights. Somewhere where I will not be persecuted, where I can live my normal life, where I don't face death threats, where I am not discriminated against on a daily basis. I would like a home where am treated like a human being. I only need support and help to be removed from this place and resettled in a safer country.

Human rights mean little to me. In recent times, no one has come to fight for our human rights, apart from fighting us trying to fight for ourselves. Please, I am not ready to lose my life. I have seen many lives perishing. It's better to die of sickness and not to be murdered, burned alive, like my friend was who was attacked by another human being who sees us like a devil. I am a normal person like others. I want to live a better life. I need to be rescued from this death trap.

Clair asks her LGBTQIA+ friends in Australia to support her and the children in Kakuma: https://www.gofundme.com/f/help-for-claire-and-her-neighborss

Refuge in Sweden
PURITY

'We win together. Let's not forget vulnerable people as we win!'

My name is Purity, I am a transgender lady originally from Uganda. I have spent five years in Kenya since 2016 to January 2021, where I saw many LGBTQ+ persons get tortured, arrested, some getting lynched and killed. I personally got arrested many times and was always living in tension in fear of the worst happening.

It is hard to seek asylum in Kenya. I faced many so challenges of transphobia. I had to get resettled to Sweden, where I stay now.

My difficulties go back to the fact that I am a transgender activist and very visibly known, both in Kenya and Uganda, and so it was so easy for me to be picked on. That's why the UNHCR had to resettle me faster, and although it took me five years, I am glad to be resettled in Sweden.

For the last twelve months, my biggest challenges have been transitioning from one country, Kenya, to a totally different country, Sweden, where I am happier and safer.

Since January of this year, I have had to adapt to a very cold country, where the culture and everything's different. The coldness, the weather is so harsh. But apart from that, before I came to Sweden, in my last days in Kenya, my life was in danger. It was my biggest challenge because as a transgender activist, I was getting known publicly. I could pretend like, getting out of the house and dress up like a man, so they would not recognise me. But people got to know who I was even when I pretend.

I tried to stay indoors almost 24/7 so I didn't get lynched out there, or risk having landlords evict me and putting me at greater risk. I was always on the move from one house to another, from hotel to another place, and feeling the hopelessness of begging to get rent, to get food, to get all the basic needs.

In Kenya, so many people beg for help, and so many people would come up with a little that they could afford to help me with food, rent, transport, medical care. Sometimes, help doesn't come through, but I was always grateful. In Kenya, many transgenders get no help and they are stuck, but for me I got help. Here in Sweden, I get enough help, and I am grateful to the Swedish people.

Transitioning has been and is such a joy and a relief from the closeted box I was trapped in, yet harder on me than anything I could imagine. I had to face up to unimaginable prejudices plus a huge price that's come with it.

Where I would love to be in the next twelve months is to use my voice and my visibility, because my voice can be heard now that I am in a safer country. I want to look out for my fellow transgenders in Kenya and Uganda, and also LGBTQ+ refugees who suffer transphobia and homophobia. I want to make sure that on every platform I am given, I advocate for them and make their plight known. They might get help if people learn about their situation. It is hard also in Kakuma refugee camp, where people are getting burnt to death for who they are. Some are committing suicide. I would love to advocate for them. And I would love to champion mental health for them, because there are so many mental breakdowns. I want their plight to be known, so they can be rescued and placed into countries that are more accepting.

Geoff Allshorn worked with Purity and Clair on these articles. Geoff is a former schoolteacher and has been a member of many LGBT and other community/activist groups. Geoff's writing can be found in previous issues of *Bent Street*.

We can help support local and overseas LGBTIQA+ refugees and asylum seekers through groups and projects such as:

- https://chuffed.org/project/humans-in-need-rainbow-refugees
- www.manycolouredsky.org.

A Night on the Town
MEL ROMERO

Please, please, come!

His voice pleaded insistently, urgently over the phone.

There's a bus you can catch right there, outside the airport. I'll be waiting for you by the office when you get here. I miss you so much, and I need to see you again. Please, come. I want you here.

The flight had been long. Seven hours and the seats wouldn't recline properly. It was a cheap flight after all. Not even water had been served. As soon as I landed, I sought the bus stop. It was right outside one of the side doors; easy to find, alluring in its invitation.

– Excuse me, where do you buy tickets?

– Don't worry mate, they're never full and you can get'em on board.

By the time a modern bus arrived it was already dark. The front seat, on the row across from the driver, was empty. I took it as a good omen. I put the bag in the seat next to mine and tried to get comfortable. It was impossible. The space was too small for my legs. My knees were squashed against the hard front. At least it was better than the plane's.

A lurch and we are on the move. A slight drizzle is turning the front lights into a million little stars that blur the view of the rapidly approaching highway. I close my eyes, but sleep won't come. My head feels heavy, and I have a nagging pulse in the back of my skull.

It's only three hours and you'll be here. You'll stay at my place, and we'll forget the past and we'll talk, and everything will be fine again!

The bus quickly gathers speed. There is barely any traffic going our way. The suburbs quickly disappear, and night envelops us. Beyond the circle of car lights, nothing can be seen. Tree shadows punctuate the mostly open fields that surround us. They can be divined but not seen. I stare out of the window, into the night, until my eyes hurt. Again, I try to sleep.

I am too tired. Sleep evades me. The past keeps playing over and over in my mind. Images, memories, sights – like an endless series of shorts, with me as an unwilling spectator, trapped in this moving theatre. More trees, more fields, endless emptiness speeds by. The repetition is hypnotic, a silent symphony being played just for me. Three seats back someone is gently snoring. A petrol station flashes by – an oasis of light quickly gone.

I check the time. One more hour and I'll be there. I have been travelling since early morning. Almost 18 hours since I left my bed. My body hurts, my muscles are cramped, but it's only one more hour. I'm almost there. I have made it. I'll be … we will be back, and the past will melt away. Years, fights, angry words, distances will all vanish as if they never were.

I shift my weight around for the hundredth time. Lights from the oncoming traffic keep on hurting my eyes. We go by what must be either a huge plain, or a very calm lake. Difficult to tell in the dark. My watch tells me we must be very near the city, but there are still no houses, no lights to be seen. Only the tarmac, in front of us, stretching like a black welcoming carpet. The rest of the world is just emptiness. Soon it will be 11 pm. We should be there any time now.

The city appears suddenly as from nowhere. It seems formed out of broad avenues, low buildings, and lots of empty space. There's not a single car around. The bus starts to brake gently and flows smoothly over the perfectly aligned streets. It just rolls on and on without a sound. Now it is slipping into a parking lot. This is it. We're here.

The people get off without a single word being spoken. They look tired, haggard under the harsh streetlights, and silently they melt away into the quiet night. Not a murmur is heard. A silent dance without music. I look around for his face, but there's nobody here. The bus driver just locks the door, nods once to me, and walks towards the only parked car. He gets in and drives away. Just as suddenly as I arrived, I'm alone in an empty city that looks as empty as a battlefield after the battle. I look around again, but still, there's nobody here.

I take my bag and sit on the curve. Here I am in a strange city – a strange, vacant city – in a strange country. The silence is deafening. Nobody is around to ask directions from even if I knew where I am supposed to go. The buildings are all dark. A slightly cold wind blows, threading its way around the treeless space. The sky is remarkably clear. Thank God for small mercies: at least it is not raining. That would have been the perfect touch to cap this movie noir.

I take out my phone and dial him. I let it ring until the voice mail comes on. Once, twice, three times. I leave no message. What is there to say?

So, what now? By the empty looks, this is a business district, and it doesn't seem to have a hotel in sight. Neither is any taxi cruising for passengers who could take me to one. The bus-office window informs me that they will be open again for business by 6am. I check: it is close to midnight. This is supposed to be a safe city, but who knows what is considered safe anymore anywhere? The silence is not comforting.

I feel the need to walk. The air seems all too thin. I cannot remain immobile. My body claims exercise after so many hours cramped. Sleep is all gone. I recheck my travel notes. There is an address there. An old and outdated address: his first address here. He doesn't live there anymore, but through our endless conversations and the pictures he sent me I came to know that place intimately. I have six hours to kill, and I need to move. That address is as good as any for a visit tonight. Seven kilometres away. I can go there and be back in time to leave by the first bus.

I program the route on my phone, shoulder my bag and start walking. The main avenue ends soon in a roundabout and a bridge. I go over what seems to be a lake with large park slopes on its shore. As soon as I get to the other side, the map directs me to the right, towards a dark clump of trees. I pause, gathering courage. The place looks empty. There are no streets lights there, not even a house to run for help if help be needed. Tsch … I'm on a mission, so I take a breath and soldier on.

The roads winds and curves and follows along the shore of the lake and finally stops being a road at all. Now it is just a dirt track across a dark hill. I continue slowly. There is no moon out, so I keep on tripping on the uneven ground. I go down on a hidden rock. I can feel a slow burn and trickle down my leg. Just another irritation to add to the long list – one more link in an endless chain going back through ages.

Finally, there are some lights. It is an empty construction site. Beyond the brambles and the gravel, a paved street can be seen and some proper streetlights. Houses are fairly big. It must be a wealthy area. That one has a foreign flag … and that other one too!

Well, the map is clear: up that road, left here, right at the corner. Up a hill, down a slope, at the further end I come to another highway heading out of town. As I walk, my body seems to move on its own, while my mind is back replaying endless memories in a constant loop.

Is this where all the love I invested took me to: an empty road stretching out forever?

I walk on. My brow is sweaty, but my body is cold. Walking drives the cold away. A mild breeze is blowing. The phone starts to ring. I don't even bother to check it. Only one person has this number. I keep on walking. Now between the rings of the calls, the pings of the messages start to abound. I turn the sound off. Nothing good comes from looking back.

On and on. Another bridge, another overpass comes and goes. Another dark park. The map says I must be getting close. Yes, that's the street name, but where is the number? I go to the very end – it's a short street after all – but numbers do not match. I must have gone too far. I reverse my steps. That small two-storey building must be it. I remember he lived in a second floor. He used to walk to a nearby bus stop … there's a bus stop over there. Yes, this is it! The building is unobtrusive, much smaller than expected – but what memory, long sought, doesn't turn out smaller that we remember or imagined?

Slowly, tiredly, I climb the stairs and softly touch the outside of his former door. It is three-thirty AM: middle of the night, or maybe just early morning? Who cares? I made it. I arrived. Long ago I promised that I would visit him here, and here I am. I have kept my word.

I sight deeply. The air feels lighter and warmer. A weight has been lifted and I am so very tired now. I sit on a low wall by the parking area, across from his place, trying to imagine him coming out. What would I say? How would I look? Maybe I would just embrace him and let it be. There's not a sound anywhere. Even the wind has quieted. I hope nobody sees me lurking about and decides to call the police.

I pull my phone and take a couple of pictures. When you date a habitual liar, you get used to providing proof to back your every word. On a whim, I post them online. There are thirty-seven messages and miscalls. Thirty-seven! Who would believe it? I stretch and yawn. I need to start walking back. I cannot let sleep overtake me, or my muscles get cold. I must keep on moving. If I walk at the same pace, I will make it right on time to catch the six o'clock back, and then I can sleep in the bus.

Traffic on the highway is starting to pick up. I'm confined to walking on the bike path by the side of the road. A few cars zoom by. I am so tired. The bag is weighing heavily on my back. Keep walking, just keep walking. Another car is coming from behind. It is honking, getting closer and honking furiously … Keep walking, just keep walking. Don't look back … There's a bus to catch.

I am a fifty-five-year-old Chilean currently working towards his PhD. In my life I've lived in 12 countries, visited another 20, attended 10 different universities and worked in all 5 continents. Packing and unpacking are second nature to me. In my writings I try to recapture those small, evanescent, personal memories that come to mind late at night, when I'm in bed trying to sleep and sleep won't come.

image: Jamie James

Kay (with Indi)

she her

What makes me thrive besides the usual? The people I love and my pets. There is nothing to compare with going fast on motorcycles, cars or boats. It's the best way to know I'm alive …

I COULDN'T GET ENOUGH OF SHARING MYSELF WITH THE WORLD MY FIRST SHOT. AND SECOND. AND TWENTY-FOURTH. THE SCRATCHY, SCRUBBY BEGINNINGS OF FACIAL HAIR. EVERY TIME I GOT SOMETHING NEW THING WITH MY CHOSEN NAME ON

Visibility and Exhaustion
BRYSON CHARLES

Sometime last year, at a pub, I told a bunch of people I was trans.

And felt … gross.

It was like I'd lost a part of myself. Instead of that rush, that new sense of connection and friendship, I was just tired.

On the train home that night, I felt diminished. Smaller.

For a long time, telling people of my experience as a trans man was a point of pride. A triumphant declaration of *me*. I relished in it. Revelled in it.

I couldn't get enough of sharing myself with the world.

My first T shot. And second. And twenty-fourth. The scratchy, scrubby beginnings of facial hair. Every time I got some new thing with my chosen name on it. Ties. Haircuts. Being called 'young feller'.

Rocking back in his squishy brown chair with a knitted blanket draped over it, fixing me with his steady gaze, a friend and mentor of mine pointed out that maybe one day, I wouldn't want everyone to know.

'No way', I said, a mixture of irritation and amusement rising in me. 'I'll never not want people to know'.

How could I not? This was my greatest achievement, the very distillation of my essence. How could I not want everyone to know, every second of every day? The idea of them *not* knowing seemed almost...rude. A disservice to myself.

But as time wore on, there *were* things I didn't want to share.

I didn't want to share the intensely personal, painful, joyful, journey of top surgery. That privilege was reserved for a select few.

I didn't want to share the frustrating tangle of cross-state issues I navigated to change my birth certificate. If I disclosed the barriers to getting 'male' on my birth certificate, would people then think about what it had once said?

The 'further' down the path of transition I walked, the less comfortable I became with any association with my past presentation.

Also, the burdens and battles began to feel more and more like mine, and less like stories to be shared. They were only for those who understood. My siblings in arms.

Gradually, it became so that sharing felt less like I was giving myself to others, and more that I was being taken away. Taken apart.

When you choose to be openly trans, there comes a point where you realise you're everybody's go-to. When you have shared so much of yourself, you set a precedent of being emotionally available to people. You lose your sense of privacy, and you start to view your existence as a mission.

The night at the pub, where I told a group of people for whom I'd just run a workshop aimed at forming connections among queer men, was a real turning point. The exhaustion, the depletion, surprised and upset me.

So I decided I'd be less open. That I'd be more strategic. I decided I would tell new people less often, and not post about it on Facebook.

I hoped it would not be as exhausting, that I would feel fortified.

And it was, in some ways. It is. I feel empowered to stand as an ally in ways I didn't before. I feel good moving through the world as someone who has more control over his own story.

But I also feel a loss. And burdens. And guilt. And questioning.

I feel the loss of immediate camaraderie that comes with disclosing automatically to other trans folks.

I feel the loss of bringing my whole self to new situations.

I feel the burden of having to omit, withdraw, edit when talking about my past. The burden of wondering if my voice is too high, if I am too short, if I am too...feminine.

I feel guilt at not being as out and proud as I once was. Am I being a 'bad queer'?

And the question that always buzzes away in my mind is when to tell? If I haven't told someone the first time I meet them, when *is* the right time? The second time? The twenty-fourth?

The fact is, in or out, I lose either way.

But in those losses, there are gains, too.

Being out, there is the joy of sharing. And of giving.

And being in, there is immense privilege. There is time. There is breathing space.

I have the privilege of thinking about how and why I am sharing such personal information. Sometimes it's to educate. Sometimes it's an act of solidarity. Sometimes it's to fuck shit up. Sometimes it's to have a closer relationship with someone.

At the end of it all, I remind myself that I am so lucky to have this choice. That there are trans folks who can never ask themselves the question, because they can never be out. Or they don't have passing privilege.

For their sake, I hope I can use my disclosure strategically, powerfully.

I hope I can use it to make a difference.

I *will* use it to make a difference.

The last time I was at a pub, I was with a bunch of new friends. Only one of them knows I'm trans.

The whole night, I kept wondering if I should tell them. The familiar, thrumming question. I decided not to.

I am learning to let go of the obligation I feel to be publicly trans. I hope that by letting go, visibility will once again be a joy. A triumphant declaration.

After all, that's what it should be.

Bryson is a proud bi trans man. He enjoys podcasts, period dramas, & hot drinks. Writing was, and is, a key part of understanding & affirming himself. He would like to thank Ursula and Sparrow, as well as the members of 'Spilling the T', especially Sam & Yves. His future plans include finishing his degree, advocacy, and writing.

in-cis-ions
GOOD JUDY

Cis parents *when I* trans-ition will *your* in-cis-ions make you Mum & Dad

...or **Dumb & Mad?**

Cis sister *when I* transition
will *your* in-cis-ions be
to
Calling Me Mister

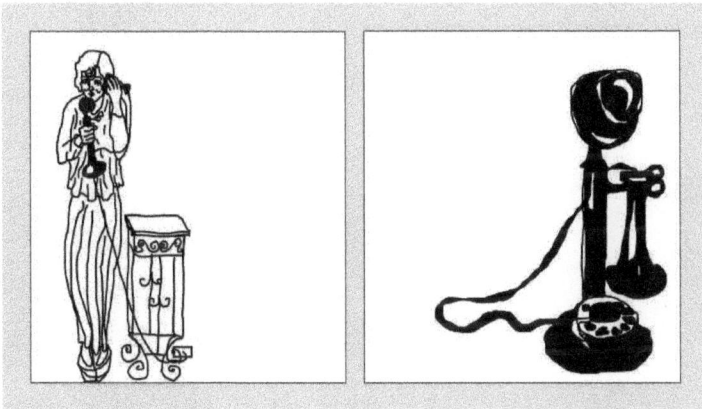

...or make me
**Miss Her
Calling?**

Already some cis pals made their de-cis-ions!

From Go Alongs

to **Long Agos**

My hound instead
trans-planted,

from **My
Backyard
Garden**

...to **Guarding
My Back**

Cis media
made in-cis-ions, from
News Ltd.
Newspapers

...to **Limited**

New

Loo-papers

Fam, make your in-cis-ions in that 'Godly' part of you,

that Cuts-Off...

& feed it to that steadfast Dogly heart of you, as

Off-Cuts

good judy is an artist, trans-girl, greyhound-lover, arts major and twenty-going-on-1920s diva. She enjoys playing around with spoken word and with digital media, graphite, and soft pastels. This is her first submission of her work to a publication. She aims at more!

This is my Story
STACEY STOKES

Hello, my name was John. I remember a couple of things from when I was a little one. One is pretty fire, the other is a pretty dress. I was 'pretty' impressed with them both, since they both stuck in my little head forever.

So, as a toddler, I set fire to the lounge room, and started dressing in my sister's old clothes. I was taught both were very wrong and should not be done.

Fire hurts people and poor little animals' homes are destroyed. So, I stopped playing with fire. But I still liked girls' clothes and pretty pink things. I played with the girls when I was in prep and primary school and went to their birthday parties. But I was still made to feel that I was doing the wrong thing. I couldn't understand why.

When I was told that me dressing like a girl was wrong, I wondered why? No one was being hurt. The only ones hurting anyone were the people calling me a poofter. The only ones getting hurt were the people on Jerry Springer getting bashed for being transgender. It was really confusing, and I lost trust in society. I didn't know who to trust or who to listen to.

All my life, I've been told not to lie. I've also been told not to act like a sissy or a poofter. But I am transgender. To act masculine, I must lie. Isn't lying wrong? But so am I. I am wrong. That's how I learnt to lie. Maybe this is why so many transgender people have mental health issues, or are in jail.

It's hard to do the right thing when you are the wrong thing.

And so began the long journey of being alone and feeling lost.

So, I tried being a boy, but I think the boys could see I was faking it since none of them wanted to be my friend. By about Year 3, I didn't want to be at school anymore. I felt like a loser and a liar. So, I stopped going. I pretended I was sick, or I just refused. Everyone was exasperated and didn't know what to do with me. Eventually, a truant officer came around and took me to school. I'd go with them so that my Mum didn't get into trouble. Then, I'd walk into the school and straight out the other side.

High school was better. Being thin and having long hair, I just looked like an emo, or someone in a Metal band. I started listening to

Metallica and Tool. I still made friends with the girls, and the guys thought I was an 'epic player' who was sleeping with them all. My female friends would play with my 'beautiful' long hair and would dress me up as a 'joke'. I got a girlfriend too, who would sometimes leave her clothes at my place. I'd secretly wear them, which made me feel normal.

Being a teenager is hard anyway, but I was torn about how to express myself. I didn't know how to be an authentic version of me. Who was I? My girlfriend helped me decide. I guess she had found someone just like her dear daddy, who she said had gotten a sex change and run away. She told me I had to cut off all my hair because it upset her.

And so began the long journey of overcompensating

I did everything society and television told me to do. I got married to a beautiful woman and had two gorgeous children with her. I got a job in security as it was super manly. I had also applied to the defence force, but was worried I wouldn't fit in, so I rejected my offer when I received it. I started working out and got my motorcycle licence. I even grew facial hair. People seemed proud of me. I was proud that I'd finally done something right.

I began to think 'This is my life now. Forever, until I die. I will never be happy. I am trapped in a lie. Forever. I will never get to be an authentic person. I will never get to be me.' All these thoughts turned incredibly toxic and seeped into every facet of my life. Physically, I developed an eye twitch, started to grind my teeth, and I felt that my throat was closing over. But mentally, I projected my unhappiness on everyone around me, taking the path of least resistance, and hurting those I loved in mean and passive aggressive ways. Part of me knew it was happening and I wished I would die every day. I added nothing but sadness to the world. I'd pray to make it all stop to anyone that would listen. At the time I didn't think so, but my prayers were finally answered when I was walking through the car park where I worked and police surrounded me and stuffed me into a police van. What happened and why is another story for another time. But, what is relevant to the story is that I eventually got bail. Due to my charges, I lost my security licence and hence, my job. I was also given an order to stay away from my family as well. So, no job, no wife, no kids, no house. I had built myself up as an avatar of masculinity, my whole unhappy existence was based on this. And now it was gone. Who I was, was gone.

This left me deeply traumatised. I couldn't function anymore. I stayed with my mum and nan and carried around a teddy bear from my childhood. I had cracked up. In retrospect, I believe I had gotten to this point due to fear of making hard choices. Being scared of being an outcast, and fearing my family would be embarrassed by me. It was all on me. Just a coward.

I was an empty husk and ghosted through lawyer's meetings, police check ins, court hearings and counselling every week. I was told every time that I was in a lot of trouble. I spent every day thinking 'I'm screwed.' I was a ghost with only one thought. I'm screwed. This was my new identity, my new me.

And so began the ghostly journey of Mr Screwed

Drowning and desperate, I was willing to do anything, no matter how fanciful, to make it alright. So, I Googled 'Sell soul'. I didn't need my soul anymore. I was an empty husk, and in my mind, I was going to hell anyway. While Googling this, I got a job as a cleaner in a supermarket. Maybe 'sell' and 'soul' was in their keyword search, some supermarkets stock pretty much everything! Or maybe I had succeeded, and I now cleaned Hell's deli and produce aisle. Either way, I was now employed, and I still wasn't sure how to sell my soul. eBay maybe?

I really liked cleaning, a job you can do on autopilot. It paid pretty good and living with mum and nan, I had leftover money. Since it was hammered home constantly that I was screwed, I didn't even consider saving any money and focused on retail therapy. So, what to buy for retail therapy? Pretty dresses! I was alone and screwed anyway. I didn't think it would bother anyone since I was in my own room and the toilet attached was pretty private.

It made me happy, like a little bit of light shining in the darkness. In a strange way, I was facing prison, but I felt free and liberated by just being me. I wish I had my own place so I could dress in my beautiful girls clothes all day, and sleep in a nightie. The only downside was that I didn't feel my body matched my clothes. I would stand in front of the mirror and judge myself. Take pictures and examine them with a critical eye. I would decide I needed to get surgery on this and that. But it was nice to express and explore who I am.

I spent my time Googling being trans and taking surveys online. All the surveys said I had gender dysphoria. I already knew I wanted to be a girl, but putting a name on it was really eye-opening. I didn't feel as much like a freak. But still, what would my family think? My friends? Maybe I would be found not guilty at trial, and I could go back to being an unhappy man. I didn't want to be anything but normal. Society had already shown me I wouldn't be accepted, so I was scared.

In the end, it didn't matter anyway. The jury found me guilty, and John died. I was now a villain, an outcast. Society does not give second chances; you do your time and keep your conviction that you must mention in every job interview. Each time a car is stolen in your area, the police visit you first. I was scum. So, I embraced who I really wanted to be, and if people thought I was a freak, well, that was better than being a villain. Nothing to lose anymore, I had lost it all being a coward already.

In brief, I informed my lawyers I had gender dysphoria. I was assessed by a clinical psychologist. I was diagnosed with gender dysphoria, and the judge accepted this.

Then I was sent to a men's prison on hormone tablets. But that's another story.

And so began the long journey of Stacey. To be continued.

Stacey Stokes is a trans woman who is currently incarcerated. She enjoys playing music, letter writing and pursuing creative writing. She says that her writing is 'a little window out of the hell of being a female in a men's prison.'

Teague Leigh

An Image of Teague
TEAGUE LEIGH

The wind is whipping up sand at me and my camera. I try desperately to protect the body (the camera's and my own). I'm with my support worker on a secluded beach on Phillip Island. I couldn't be happier, despite the ferocious 80km per hour winds. Images of rock formations and moody clouds fill up my mind, and my hard drive. Seascapes remedy a cracked soul. Nature stirs something primal in me; something organic. My skin tingles. It's not just due to the cold.

I learnt photography back in year 11 and 12. Way back, like … way back. I'm talking pre-digital, dark-room days. The smell of chemicals singeing the nostril hairs as you processed your snapshots. Even back then I focused on nature and animals – there are plenty of horses in the paddocks around Canberra. I've never understood portrait work. People are so difficult. I guess that's my autistic sensibilities. Even now, my photographs are primarily *sans* people. Except when I volunteer my services for the Melbourne Queer Film Festival, which allows me to be around crowds without the stress and anxiety of an unfiltered experience.

I am an empath, but the autism makes it difficult to immediately process. In my twenties, my creative muse wouldn't leave me alone. The photography of my teenage years was left behind for epic poems and sex-laden prose, delving deep into my experiences with would-be lovers. So much richer and deeper than the bad poetry of my childhood. I performed my cunning linguistics at queer spoken word nights around Canberra, and then at festivals and conferences around the country. I became a published writer and performed alongside world-renowned authors. Writing was my life, and it looked like it would take me places.

I moved to Melbourne and continued to be compelled by a muse that had so much to say. I spoke at community events at Hares and Hyenas and was published in more anthologies. But even a muse is not indestructible.

I had long been working part-time in soulless corporate jobs within the banking and insurance industries, which made me dread waking up each day. I have always struggled with depression, on and off medications. It creeps like death itself.

Transitioning helped curb much of the darkness. Twelve years ago I had chest surgery, and it literally saved my life. The burden of wearing three layers of clothing to hide my body in 35 degree heat was stifling. Never seeing myself in the mirror the way I envisioned was dysphoric. The surgery alleviated the dysphoria and in the warmth of the summer days I was able to take my shirt off at the beach for the first time in three decades. The light breeze tickling my newly formed nipples was a thrill. I felt carefree again, like when I was a breastless child.

However, chest surgery also led to me getting fired. My employer thought my transition would make the bathrooms too difficult to navigate for the rest of the firm.

My then partner pushed me to get a full-time job, to '*contribute to society*'. Three months into an insurance position, our tumultuous three-year relationship ended badly when she believed rumours over my own truth. I was kicked out of the house and banned from seeing her children who had become a large part of my life. Cut off, and without closure, I was distraught. Through all of this, writing was the only highlight in my life. Thank the Mother for my words and the outlet they provided me. I filled countless notebooks with trans masculine and gay male erotica. I kept my drafts to myself. I only submitted to callouts when I felt the pieces had real merit.

Three years into that job of mindless paperwork and endless data-processing, I was hiding my trans identity in the hyper masculine corporate world. I had no true friends because of the difficulties I face with my autism. I was alone. I had unfulfilling affairs and one-night stands with men and women I met on Scruff and Pink Sofa. None of them felt significant, as the trauma I'd been through was still too raw. The idea of a relationship of any length filled me with dread.

I was breaking. I couldn't hear my muse, but I could hear hornets or wasps outside my window. I no longer wrote at all. Then, mysterious bumps started appearing all over my body. My GP initially thought they were bug bites, so I sterilised my home constantly with industrial strength bug spray. The acrid chemicals singed my nostril hairs. For months the 'bites' colonised my body. Itching drove me to distraction. I'd lose time looking at specks of dust, wondering if they were the bugs that were biting me. I spent thousands of dollars on a pale stale male dermatologist who would take multiple punch biopsies to determine the cause of my affliction in his pale stale office. Then there were the chemicals he prescribed me. Bitter pills, scrubs and body washes. All to no effect.

Changes at work increased the stress I was under. Procedure timing and monitoring, introduction of KPIs as well as new management and office address with standing hot desks. My autism does not appreciate change. I eventually told my manager – who was younger than I was – that the workplace either had a bug infestation or I was going crazy. That blonde and incompetent man laughed at me and did nothing. I felt invisible and forsaken.

I treated myself to a soothing bath of Epsom salts one night after work. Instead of relaxation, it led to the sensation of electrification, and I rushed to hospital panicking about the lesions on my skin. I told the triage nurse that I might be contagious. Then I sat waiting for hours in a secluded room. I'd wrapped myself up head to toe in layers of jeans, long sleeved tee and ski jacket in the middle of summer, and spun glad wrap around my head to trap the bugs in. Two doctors and a nurse examined me, but they sent me home without a solution.

After that night, my GP immediately referred me to a psychiatrist for evaluation. Two months later I was diagnosed with schizophrenia, despite having lived eight months with a supposed physical condition. The 'bug bites' were psychosomatic. I was prescribed more pills.

I had experienced mental illness since I was very young. The stigma of depression in the 80s and 90s was very real, but I tried my best not to let it get to me. But nothing prepared me for this. I wanted to write about it, but my brain had been damaged by mental stress. The change in my cognitive abilities shocked and appalled me. Without the writing I had nothing. I unravelled. Who was I if I couldn't write? I was known for my writing. That's how I mattered, and how I contributed to society. Right? Without words did I even matter?

Work eventually fired me as I was no longer able to turn up. I was devastated, especially as my schizophrenic episode had come on as a direct result of the stress I'd been under at work. Now, I had nothing. No job. No words. No lover. No muse.

I was alone and frightened. I couldn't concentrate. My depression intensified. My autism spiralled and I took myself out of society. Workers compensation allowed me to sleep more than I should have. I searched for flatmates I would then hide from and window shopped on eBay for things I couldn't afford.

I withdrew for months. Years. Memory loss means most of it's a blur. I fought to obtain support from the National Disability Insurance Scheme (NDIS) and after appealing my initial rejection, I won and was allowed to access supports. Schizophrenia has been a big part of my life now for nine years; I only secured NDIS funding three years ago. These supports were the tools I needed to tentatively step back into society.

I asked myself how I could be creative without being able to write anymore. I turned to a dusty, ill-used Panasonic zoom camera I had all but forgotten about. The city was accessible when I stood behind the camera. Architecture and streetscapes with their lines and curves started whispering to me. Eventually I managed to afford a Nikon DSLR and a couple of kit lenses from eBay, my wishlist finally being used. With the help of a support worker I could go on photographic expeditions to the Grampians, The Great Ocean Road and Phillip Island. Always nature. The wilder, the better. I was rusty; it frustrated me, but I have persevered.

There are moments where the stigma of living with schizophrenia makes my depression escalate. I still yearn to write. I have a new partner who is an author and he's helping me to read and write again. He helped me edit this essay, the first writing I've done in nine years. I'm grateful every day for his insights, patience and love. I'm grateful for the camera. With words still not flowing freely, the camera tells the world what I want to say.

The wind whips up at my face and I instinctively protect my camera first rather than my eyes. The sun is setting through the broken storm clouds. The rock formations pose amongst the crashing waves. I am at home here. The noise of my mental illness, depression, anxiety and even my autism is quiet here. The muse now the click of the shutter in amongst a gale, it is music to my mending soul.

Teague Leigh is an autistic trans man from planets unknown, currently residing on Wurundjeri and Bunurong Country. Once upon a time he was anthologised in various works and performed his spoken words around the country. Now he is a photographer, letting his landscape images speak for him. Find more of Teague at https://linktr.ee/tlwvision

Teague Leigh

Anastasia Le

Labels
ANASTASIA LE

F.o.b

The term I had never heard before arriving in Australia.

F.o.b. A name used to address me which had no meaning to my bilingual mind. Yet somehow, it triggered a bout of laughter in many local kids; white and non-white alike.

I came to this country by plane. I left my home at fifteen to study and eventually live here. Why did they say I came by boat?

F.o.b meant that people spoke louder and slower to me
If they bothered speaking to me at all.
F.o.b can make you useless. The ones with pigmented skin are.
They are *'not really what we are looking for'*.
But not all f.o.b are useless.

F.o.b meant I had to wake up at 3am just to go to a job that started at 5am. I had to travel sixteen kilometres by train, bus and foot to arrive there on time. My colleague (not f.o.b) who lived closer to the job could not possibly get up that early. They had an early class, you see. The same class that I attended.

You know what f.o.b really means to me? It means giving up a luxurious breakfast of phở, broken rice or steaming hot congee for some sad bread smeared with yellow goo and fruit-flavoured sugar spread. Or on a good day, a bowl of processed cereals and cold, white milk.

F.o.b and Asian somehow exist side by side. Asian means that your food is 'intriguing' but Australians eating Vegemite for breakfast should not be questioned.

Asian means that your driving is really bad.

F.o.b and Asian means that you are fantastically wealthy and you're stealing the locals' jobs.

To many, Asian now means disease spreader.

You know what I think being Asian means? It means we had a rich multi-faceted culture, and were civilised in our own ways. Until the spice road screwed us up.

Gay

I was also called Gay back in the day.

We gays were considered degenerates; morally corrupt.

Twinky gays got bashed. There was a lot of rejection. A lot of relentless competition for acceptance. I once embodied all that pain because they said I was a *twinky* gay.

Asian *twinky* gay, now that was a mouthful.

People didn't use this specific string of words to reject me.

They showed it through action.

They showed it through « masc for masc »

« no femmes »

« whites only »

They were (and possibly still are) a few of the labels to keep other labels away.

I believe the labels they affixed on me helped me somehow. They unburdened me from the masculinity and heteronormativity that was meant for me. Instead, I could show my courage and strength.

I have witnessed how labels affect everybody, not just me. Especially since I started seeing myself for who I truly am, how I was created and am meant to be. A woman.

Woman

'You need bigger tits.'

'You should stay trim.'

'Don't work out too much or you'll lose your ass.'

'You've gained weight from being on estrogen?'

Affirmation with shades of misogyny.

Before my journey to authenticity, there were many other expectations imposed on me.

Young man

'Don't be a sissy, stop crying.'

'Where's your facial hair?'

'You cook? You are certainly not straight.' (But I am straight as a woman!)

'Work hard, support your family.'
'It should be easy lifting all that heavy stuff, unless you're a girl.'
'You should have some more muscles.'
Now as a woman, I carry more.

Labels

Trans
Asian
Immigrant
Feminist

I carry all that I have experienced before one hundred times more.

Somehow, I am now a feminazi, somehow I have stopped *'understanding men'*.

Somehow, I am now a social justice warrior. Which means I have *'lost my compassion'*.

Somehow me being a woman is intimidating to some men just as me being a man would be threatening to some women.

I am caught up in the middle of a conflict

My past and my present

My lost experiences and my true authenticity.

I hear and feel all of the cries of the labels.

Labels are meant to be here to help us understand each other.

But instead, we use those labels to judge.

Humanity is so screwed up.

Anastasia Le is a Vietnamese immigrant, who has spent half of her time on the land of the Wurundjeri people. As a woman of trans experience, she's learned to use humour, her voice to raise awareness for the queer community, racial issues, and inequality. Labels was first performed at the LGBTIQA+ storytelling night 'Let me get something off my chest' at the Bowery Theatre, St Albans in April 2021.

image: Jamie James

AJ

I am who I am and by being true to me that enables me to love me ...

QUEER ME CRAZY//ALLIES (ALL-LIES?)
RUQ

Words ... words so convoluted they no longer hurt ...

Doesn't mean that I'm no longer hurt
It simply means I've gotten so used to being hurt

It doesn't mean that I'm no longer bothered
It just means I've gotten so used to feeling bothered

Normalize this pain
Say it like how you think it's 'not supposed to hurt'
Remind me of how 'if we accept ourselves as we are
we shouldn't feel ashamed'

But elucidate to me how and why wouldn't it hurt
when we know what you mean too damn well
that you had meant them as insults as you hurl
them out at those you deem as one 'of us' as abuses
Within our presence or outside of
To whomever that you think is 'deserving' of the treatment
What if the tables are turned ...?

Please,
Never fail to remind us how completely acceptable it is
to punish us throughout our entire life,
for the crime of simply being,
one that we did not even get to choose

Please,
Punish us for a life and birth that we didn't choose
and proceed on to mocking 'one of us' when they chose death
over 'coping' with this life of perpetual degradation and humiliation

Hmm … let me choose; a life of mockery or a death that is of comforting certainty

Pathologize this pain
 – extrapolate these symptoms –
 – compartmentalize them into syndromes –
 – and disorders –
 – the prodrome is perhaps our physique of having always been 'looking' so queer
 – oh and let's not forget of our 'wanting to be special/different' –

AS.FUCKING.IF

Go ahead

box us into yet another set of abnormality

Watch my face as I …

.

.

.

.

… dissociate …

.

.

.

.

Thanks
For nothing

Ruq is a sociolinguist currently studying law. A small person with big dreams: for people to be kinder and more loving to each other & themselves.

Speaking back to the binary: from isolation to community
ALEX LEE

'What is it?'

I'm standing on the school bus, bag shouldered. It's the start of year 9. I don't hope the question is not about me, I just hope they won't insist on it until everyone hears and turns to stare. Laughter. I glance over and see two girls whispering behind their hands. I bow my head against further attention. Two older boys are in front of me; there's a swagger in their stance. The blonde one smiles charmingly, 'We have a bet, will you help us?' Pause. His look and recognition of me as a 'you' grab my attention (could this be a way back to belonging?).

'Are you a girl or a boy?'

I hear my voice say 'I'm a girl' and immediately feel the self-betrayal. The boys nudge each other and turn away.

Though an ordinary scene, it is a profoundly dislocating experience. Along with the hot envelope of shame and the warp of fear, the self that arises through social exchange is tearing away from the internal map of who I am. In my gender ambiguity, I am 'it' – not fully human. To return to recognition as 'you' I must choose between two narrow options, neither of which expresses my felt sense of self. I am not just a person by being there with everyone else; rather, my humanity is conditional on the legibility of my gender.[1]

This recurrent scene fuels a tangle of questions that will come to shape my life.

How did I get to be outside and between the binary where the reigning logic is otherwise?

How am I possible?

How can I refuse this question?

Why am I the focal point for the fear, disgust and rage of strangers?

How can I make a liveable zone for me across/between boy/girl?

---

[1] Butler 17

They're questions I struggled with alone while my peers seemed to be busy building functional worlds, bound by economies of masculinity and femininity. I want, at last, to speak back to all those who asked me.

I'm not a boy; I'm not a girl

Yet I do have attributes of both. Whence this multiplicity? The culture proliferates gender-coded qualities. Myriad genres make gender as an array of feeling-investments, attitudes, behaviours, objects, modes of relation and capacities. At thirteen, my understanding of gender was beyond what I could say. It was comprised of feelings and textures: a pull towards this and not that, a sense of what felt right and good here, but not there. Shrinking from the casual violence of my peers, I turned to the school library, and discovered that literature provides a rich language of gender and invites us to immerse ourselves in the pleasures of identification.

William Godwin's 1794 novel *Caleb Williams* was written in the midst of debates about the French Revolution, as a critique of aristocratic ideals of masculinity.

> He was a common soldier, of a most engaging physiognomy … He had been ardent in the pursuit of intellectual cultivation … He was plain and unaffected … His habits of thinking were strictly his own, full of justice, simplicity, and wisdom […] His judgement was penetrating and manly … while at the same time there was such an uncontending frankness in his countenance.[2]

'He' possesses both an unassailable moral strength and a kind of sensual tenderness which I want. This is a man whose body is all surfaces and gestures; his abstract purity is a safe retreat for me. His gendering appears invested with the 'erotics of political fellowship' – that which bonds men.[3] I discover there is a welcome homoeroticism at the very heart of manliness. And more: he holds the daring extravagance and embodied fullness of the woman, is somehow necessary to her luscious multivalence.

---

[2] Godwin 179 & 191.
[3] Berlant 110.

Was she beautiful or not beautiful? And what was the secret of form or expression which gave the dynamic quality to her glance?[4]

I learn that the English novel has endowed her with the richness of our inner lives and all that goes on 'in private' – our intimacies and reflections, the textures of small daily experience – in all its involution, range, subtlety and voluptuousness. This gorgeously embellished feminine self offers a seduction to the masculine subject.[5]

> It was just then that he saw the tree, that he was conscious of its presence just inside a garden gate [...] Then from within its depths or from beyond there came the sound of a woman's voice. A woman was singing. The warm untroubled voice floated upon the air, and it was all part of the silence as he was part of it... Deep, deep, he sank into the silence, staring at the tree and waiting for the voice that came floating, falling, until he felt himself enfolded.[6]

She makes for him a transitional space, where the suppression of his body gives way to this floating dreamy sensuality. I begin to sense a zone I could inhabit: one that shifts between clearly defined genders; where their traces are in the eroticism of subjectivity and in the coupling of feminine/masculine that is detached from 'man' and 'woman'.

I won't be addressed like that anymore

It's 1999 in Perth. I've found an archive of queer possibilities; I'm studying feminism and reading Judith Butler, who writes 'gender is an 'act', as it were, that is open to splittings, self-parody, self-criticism'[7]. With these resources, surely, I might venture to live how I choose.

I use the White Pages to look up a plastic surgeon. He is a middle-aged, white man, plain and clean-shaven, with round glasses, his thinning hair cut close. Full of the confidence of my women's studies classes, I sit down and come straight to the point: 'I would like a double mastectomy'. His face tightens.

---

[4] Eliot 3.
[5] Armstrong 225.
[6] Mansfield 201-202.
[7] Butler 146-147.

After the physical exam, we return to his office, where he explains to me that my request is 'not normal'. I ask him to clarify just what he means. He takes out a piece of paper and draws the two axes of a graph, then the shape of a large steep-sided hill. 'This is a bell curve,' he says. He cuts off the two little flat tails on each side of the curve with vertical lines, 'Most people are here inside the curve'. I think: Is this guy fucking serious? I glare at him and make some sort of protest. 'You need to see a psychiatrist for five years before I will see you again,' he finishes with the resolution of a man who knows what he's about and will no longer be trifled with.

The DSM-IV, with its definition of 'gender identity disorder', is only five years old at this time. Behind it is the DSM-III, which offers a 'diagnosis' of my situation with the term 'transsexualism'[8]. Such institutional discourses purport to deal in reality, via the authority of science. By that logic, they are univocal. That the change in the DSM criteria is born of activist interventions is effaced in the document, for this would tell us all clearly that these terms are zones of politics, not truth. The surgeon's diagram represents not only the proper contours of femininity, but the zone of intelligibility operating inside medical discourse. Although these lines read to me as the surgeon marking the limits of his own knowledge, it is my agency and embodied self-extension that are constrained by them.

I begin to feel caught in a loop

'Are you a boy or a girl?' will recur in countless situations. An iteration that is at once mundane and peculiarly shaming is the public bathroom. Here the two options – man or woman – shape spaces and how our bodies can move through them.

I'm at the cinema and I need to pee. Again, this dilemma, so I choose the dingy public restroom at the end of the arcade. I walk through the door marked 'Women' (is that the right choice tonight?). A middle-aged woman gives me a second look as I enter the cubicle. I'm sitting, trousers bunched around my knees, legs open. Suddenly she is banging on the door; it shakes on its hinges: 'You can't be in here, you have to leave!' My pee stops midstream; I say nothing, hurriedly pulling up my pants. I stand there breathing shallow, listening, waiting for her to go. She bangs and yells again, and then walks out.

---

[8] Drescher 115.

As Jack Halberstam notes, for all her aggression, it's unlikely this woman actually felt physically endangered.[9] Rather, she has experienced a tremor in her perception: 'when bodies arrive that seem 'out of place,' it involves *disorientation*: people blink and then look again'.[10] The co-extensiveness of her embodiment and the gendered space gets shaky. Her world is aligned to the icons on the toilet door: '*man* and *woman* as nouns'.[11] Meanwhile, I have bent my mind to read the little triangle of 'Woman' not as a skirt, but as a daring flare that shows up the limits of the straight-edged icon on the door further down. I have hoped there would be room in this space for the not-(cis)man; thus, I have made the space queer: 'When bodies 'arrive' that don't extend the lines already extended by spaces, then those spaces even appear 'slantwise' or oblique'.[12] This woman intuits this and will not stand for it. Through our encounter, she has pushed her own unease out and away and, by the biopsychosocial rhythms of shared human life, has lodged it in my body.

The world slowly wears me down

Through the chance of time, place and community, I lived thirty-six years with no name for my experience. It felt like a unique and shameful secret, and was profoundly isolating. In 2013, the DSM-V introduced the term gender dysphoria, defined as 'discomfort or distress that is caused by a discrepancy between a person's gender identity and that person's sex assigned at birth (and the associated gender role and/or primary and secondary sex characteristics)'.[13] This, at last, explains why, when I look in the mirror, I sometimes feel strangled by self-hatred. But what the DSM does not say is what those three decades have taught me: that the sense of discrepancy is a product of the social environment. In the encounters with my peers, medical professionals and strangers I show up as myself and am met by fear and aggression. They all construct a contradiction I don't see and shame me for it. They tell me I am somehow fundamentally wrong in a way that defies reason and merits disgust:

---

[9] Halberstam 22.
[10] Ahmed 135.
[11] Butler 24.
[12] Ahmed 135.
[13] World Professional Association for Transgender Health 5.

The woman in the bathroom: 'What are you *doing* here?'

The surgeon: 'What are you *saying*?'

The boys on the bus: 'What even *are* you?'

These are only examples of some of the countless micro- (and macro-) aggressions that gender diverse people live with. Research has now linked such experience to higher rates of poor mental health, disability and complex chronic conditions among the gender diverse community.[14]

For me these manifest as: a history of suicidal ideation and self-harm; anxiety and depression; low self-esteem; a fear that lives inside me and jumps up in relationships and social spaces; a degenerative autoimmune disease; chronic pain, as the danger signalling of the brain-body become super-efficient. Gender dysphoria gives a name to the psychological pain, the self-aversive emotions and corollary sensations that come up in a person when something about gender feels incongruent. It also flags how the gender diverse person takes the discomfort of heteronormative culture inside them, so their psyche, as well as their musculoskeletal, immune and nervous systems become inscribed with it.

I *can* be both/neither

My world finally starts to open and change and I realise that there are other people who are both/neither, between and across. Now, in community spaces, I allow myself to explore what feels 'like me' I'm trying to steer close to the pleasure and respond to and move with the people around me, but trouble still arises.

At a trans masc peer support meeting, my brain stages this argument with itself:

Amygdala: Alert! Alert!

Prefrontal cortex: Now what?

Amygdala with the help of hippocampus: MEN!!!

Prefrontal cortex: As a perjorative?! We've moved on from that scheme of safety/danger. These are our people...

Amygdala-hippocampus: Humans with deep voices and beards — bad memories!!!

---

[14] Downing & Przedworski 339-343.

Prefrontal cortex: You know, maybe I want a deeper voice and a beard
...

Amygdala-hippocampus: !!!

Back at me-level, this debate registers as a flood of fearful and angry emotions and sensations meeting thoughts of connection and belonging.

On an internet date, I'm trying to cover over my anxiety by being charming and solicitous, by acting what I hope might pass for a camp version of gentlemanly. One of my preferred orientations, tonight it's also informed by how I'm reading the situation as organised around a butch/femme eroticism. The person opposite me is relating a scene in which her desire is founded; it's something about a friend from her youth whose androgynous-to-masculine look captivated her. Oh! ... Is that an outline of me? I don't want to be anyone else's fantasy anymore ... But does that mean she finds how I look – sorta-not-man – attractive? Then again, what is the sweet spot of her fantasy? Is there an underlying contract of complementarity here? Have I already consented to it? How am I to flex to and read where she wants to be in relation? Will my shifting orientation be in sync with hers?

Such movements and tensions are often confusing. The balance of gendered attributes is contingent – dependent on time, place, situation, the mesh of relations in which I am embedded, what language is being used, how and for what purpose, who is addressing me – so at any given moment, a comfort zone of how 'me' is forming may change or go out of sync with the environment. But this is what I need to explore in order to learn to be my authentic self. Sara Ahmed writes: 'Comfort is a feeling that tends not to be consciously felt', yet 'when you fidget and move around, then what is in the background comes in front of you, as a world that is gathered in a specific way. Discomfort, in other words, allows things to move'. Their own comfort is what the majority guard, and to keep their world gathered in a specific way they subject minorities to untold violence. Yet in doing so, they miss a crucial point: out of discomfort comes growth. As things jostle, one against the other, possibilities arise. I come to accept that I am not one thing, but many, and that's okay. I also learn to better see and respect others, for being a person is not about being instantly gender-legible to everyone you meet; it is this living, growing experience of difference, vulnerability, play, testing and give and take.

I can keep going cos I'm not alone

My community has taught me the courage of our sheer persistence. Even as we tussle with the constraints that operate in our worlds, we keep showing up, and this opens little utopias inside the everyday. We do this every time we use the 'wrong' bathroom, dare to dress how we want, insist on our pronouns and the names we've given ourselves. It's hard and often heartbreaking, but world transforming. We take the question I was asked and release it back into the culture: 'what is a boy, and what is a girl anyway?' We show that in the end, there are only people with bodies doing what they do in the conditions given to us, forming and reforming through our joy, love and desire.

References

Ahmed, S. (2006). *Queer Phenomenologies*. Duke UP.

Armstrong, N. (1987). *Desire and Domestic Fiction: A Political History of the Novel*. Oxford UP.

Berlant, L. (2008) *The Female Complaint*. Duke UP.

Butler, J. (1990). *Gender Trouble: Feminism and the Subversion of Identity*. Routledge.

Drescher, J. (2010). 'Transsexualism, Gender Identity Disorder and the DSM'. *Journal of Gay and Lesbian Mental Health*, 14(2) pp. 109-122. https://doi.org/10.1080/19359701003589637

Downing, J., & Przedworski, J. (2018). 'Health of Transgender Adults in the U.S., 2014–2016'. *American Journal of Preventative Medicine*, 55(3), 336-344. https://doi.org/10.1016/j.amepre.2018.04.045

Eliot, G. (2014). *Daniel Deronda*. Oxford UP.

Godwin, W. (1998). *Caleb Williams*. Oxford UP.

Halberstam, J. (1998). *Female Masculinity*. Duke UP.

Mansfield, K. (2007). *The Escape. The Collected Stories*. Penguin.

World Professional Association for Transgender Health. (2012). *Standards of Care: for the Health of Transsexual, Transgender, and Gender Nonconforming People*. https://www.wpath.org/publications/soc

Alex Lee is a trans* non-binary settler and chronically ill armchair activist who lives and works in Naarm, on the lands of the Wurundjeri people of the Kulin nations. They are currently the facilitator of a TGDNB peer support group in Melbourne and online, Trans/Gender Culture Conversation and are looking forward to starting their SPARK storytelling project, Dialoguing across Difference.

There Are No Single Stories
RYAN GUSTAFSSON

She wore an oversize pink, purple, and grey sports jacket with black slacks and runners, a look I'd seen numerous times around Namsan Tower and other outdoor destinations, always floating in pairs or large groups. Mrs Ahn, who looks so big in photographs, her hands wrapped around my torso. I heard her voice first, just moments before she materialized in the doorway of the post-adoption services room. A room thousands of others like me have walked into, hoping to walk out with something more, something different, some thing. The room where I had pressed, as gently and firmly as I could, for the release of my file. The room where I learned that what is ours isn't always ours to own.

I've grown attached to thinking in circles. Is it a question of knowledge, of knowing? Or is that beside the point? And is that the way to get to a point – to get at what's beside it? Am I not just an oblique shuffling, a wandering in spirals, a collection of different scales and rhythms?

It had been six months' worth of decisions to transition, six months of anticipation and joy, of impatience and apprehension. Six months experiencing new genres of curiosity. Examining my chin and jaw, my lips, skin, and hairline, trying to see change, trying to hold so many things at once. Before and after, below and beyond, the buried and the transformed, all unforeseeable, all stretching ahead of me. Trying to see what others might see in me.

She was so much smaller in stature than I'd expected, this woman, the only face and body that appears in documents of my past. Prior to Melbourne, with all of my new names. And I was struck by my body as flesh, my body as the measure of my growth and her transformation, and I wondered what size I was to her, how we all carry expectations in our bodies, in our skin and mouths, and that once, during a time marked by lack of memory, she would have been my entire world.

How do we trace the past, and how do we learn to recognize the traces it leaves? When are we, and how do we know? A skipping stone, or the stone that was skipped. The padding of a film of water, or the sunlight that stirs it, on a spring morning in a southern coastal city. How can we trace present absence, when it is what tears us away from ourselves, but also what hooks and bites, what arrests us?

Resemblance is a winding field and a confrontation. I think about what I am becoming and what I am losing. About what it means to resemble in the first place – what likeness is and what it means. About how to know what will be, sometimes you must also be able to see what is. About how I am always beside myself, scrambling for a perspective.

And if I look more like you, then you, too, must look more like me. A tie that is strange and disorienting, forgotten and futural, a tie for intellect only.

We took a photograph together in front of a framed map of Australia. Slightly bent, I could see bits of black hair sitting on the hood and shoulders of her jacket. Mrs Ahn, whose name I would never have uttered, having lived with her for only the first four months of my life. Who had recently had knee surgery but still decided to make the trip. Who stopped somewhere along the way, from her world to the place where she had often taken me to, for the final time over thirty years ago, to get a haircut. And as I looked at the hair that hadn't been completely brushed away, I thought about how neatness is often accompanied first by debris, by what is discarded.

To transition is to wonder. To wonder what rings through you, if only you could see it. If only you shared in something shared. To wonder if you look less like your mother, and more like your father, a father who was told you didn't make it. To wonder what you are a reminder of, and to whom. It highlights both intimacy and unbridgeable distance, a past always open to revision, and a future that may come to rewrite the present.

A week later, Mrs Ahn and her daughter take us to an amusement park along the water. All energy and movement, she can barely sit still, marching swiftly between shops and booths. She insists on buying us seafood and corndogs. She plays mini-games and wins prizes, which she shoves in my arms to take home. To Melbourne. I try to memorize the sound of her voice, to overlay memory with memory, to rediscover through immersion.

But it is her daughter who offers the quilting point, who creates a place for inhabitance. Ten years my senior, she tells me she remembers – me, an unknown other. As if she knew memory is a gift, that remembrance is sometimes the kindest form of embrace, that knowledge of us is what is held and unseen. As if she knew that to be remembered when you cannot, is to humanize. It is to furnish a view from within, to give it force, to be unstuck from the tricks I play on myself, which have allowed me to believe the only way in is as an onlooker, that the only route is through logic.

There are no single stories. I wonder how they ring through me, how they interlace and render me both more and less than what I can know.

Ryan Gustafsson is a researcher, writer, and podcaster who lives and works on Wurundjeri land. A nonbinary and adopted Korean, their writing explores themes including connection, identity, knowledge, and loss. They currently work at the Asia Institute, the University of Melbourne.

image: Jamie James

Kalypso

she her

I'm taking up space and unapologetic about it. I'm standing two feet in my truth everyday and navigating through the world ...

Telling the Truth
BLAIR ARCHBOLD

I

This edition of *Bent Street* is on trans and gender diverse issues. Well, I am a trans guy and this is my issue. I am not a fan of the comment: 'Typical cis white straight man.'

I used to live in a Brunswick share-house with housemates who would say this often, their words full of derision. I wouldn't let it be known how much I didn't like it because it was seen as the cool thing to say, and I wasn't up for the blowback I knew would come my way.

One time I must have inadvertently revealed my discomfort though because my housemate looked at me and said, 'Not you, Blair.' Not me because I'm trans, I guess.

II

So what exactly was my housemate saying? That I'm part of a small niche that is excluded from the derision (so long as I don't step out of line and challenge it). Except I'm not excluded because most people I interact with don't know I'm trans.

When I'm out in public I am perceived to be a straight white cis man and I cop the derision that is meant for them. It doesn't feel all that different from what I used to experience when I presented as a masculine woman. Judgement is judgement.

III

Some individuals on the progressive left might respond by saying that this is what minorities experience all the time, and now straight white cis men are just getting a taste of it. Except I am a part of a minority, I'm under the T in the acronym. And the next 'straight white cis man' you see walking down the street might have a disability or a history of abuse, or a mental health issue. He might actually be trans or non binary, bi, or gay. And if he's straight and cis, so what? That's not a crime, last time I checked.

And anyway, I don't want to be excluded from the derision. What was my housemate saying? That I'm not a man? Someone can't say that and call themselves my ally. I want people to see the derision for what it is.

IV

Some on the progressive left might say because I'm perceived to be a straight white cis man I'm the recipient of passing privilege. But that is not accurate either because at the end of the day I'm still trans. I still bled on an operating table to claim this body as my own.

I experience the world from a different perspective now having transitioned but there is still pain and discomfort in some of it. It is not as if now everything is perfectly fine. But it is better.

I am more comfortable in my body but I am less comfortable with the progressive left. Some people who I want to see as 'my people' now look at me with hostility. Not because they know me, but because they judge me by the colour of my skin, by my gender and by my sexuality, (all things the Left is meant to *not* judge people for).

V

I want to suggest that the strategies of calling people out and policing language do not translate well into reality, at least not in my experience. I have not seen it done in a way that isn't toxic and in my opinion that is because there is no way to intentionally shame someone that isn't toxic. Not to mention the totalitarian nature of trying to control an individual's thoughts and speech.

People have written about the cancel culture of the progressive left, drawing parallels to Mao's struggle sessions. Until recently I hadn't even heard of a struggle session, but they read as a powerful metaphor for the kind of progressive left mob mentality that plays itself out on social media, and that spills over into real life, by people who claim to value diversity and inclusivity above all else.

I know, the right side of the political spectrum does it too, with historical parallels including McCarthyism and other right wing purges. But the progressive left has more power than it realises. And does it really need to be said that two wrongs don't make a right?

VI

From my perspective both the progressive left and the conservative right are doing the same thing to each other. In the sense that they point the finger of judgement at the opposing side and fail to really look at themselves. It's a lot easier to project your dysfunction onto another than it is to self-reflect. What it results in is a failure to learn and grow.

VII

I once heard a shaman say, 'The worst kind of sorcery is the kind we do to ourselves,' and I see that as applying to the current state of the progressive left. I'm sure there is at least some good that comes out of this ideology but it is my contention there is also harm.

If the progressive left really wants to be progressive it needs to be willing to examine that as a possibility and be willing to do something about it. Because to the extent that an ideology is teaching people to turn on each other and to hate themselves it is not making the world a better place. Surely it makes sense that a better way for the progressive left to do politics is to be open to a more diverse range of ideas.

Blair Archbold has contributed writing and voiceover work as an inspiring trans community leader, including as a co-host on 3CR's *Out of the Pan: Sally Goldner and Blair Archbold*.

The 'Dreambreaker'
KATHY MANSFIELD

The Kinfolk Project, Genograms, Ripplegrams and 'the next stage' for the hearts and minds of birth families: awareness of the 'Dreambreaker' in a heteronormative society.

I am a 73-year-old Transgender Paradigm smasher, and I felt blessed to be included on the Kinfolk Project team, mentored and directed by the wonderful Dr Catherine Barrett of Alice's Garage* fame.

As I worked through the multidimensional intersections of the Kinfolk Project that became critical to a coherent project output, I was requested to develop a 'Genogram' model for my family.

While working through the required representative symbols and hierarchy inherent in the genogram tool, I found that, for me, the diagrams that were designed to assist in the family counselling context felt counter intuitive, reductionist and slightly coarse.

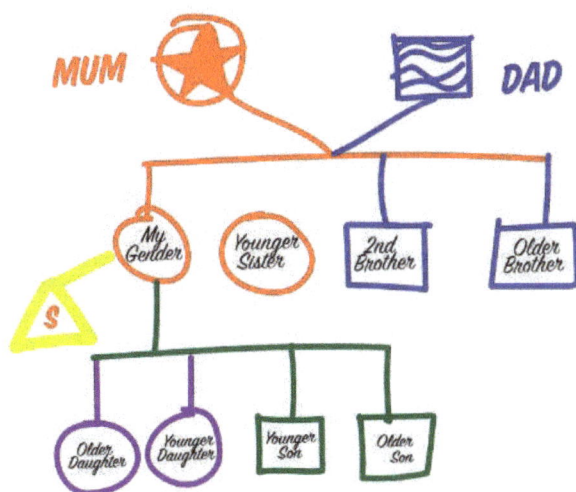

Ellie's example drawn from alicesgarage.net

When folk, from within our LGBTIQ+ spectrum communities try to engage their birth families and loved ones about their unique physical and spiritual 'inner selves', these events sometimes come as devastating shocks in traditional family structures.

I considered that a more nuanced or sophisticated framework or model was necessary to adequately describe, refine and record the highly complex range of relationships, feelings and emotion drivers that surface, at many levels. Sometimes violently and sometimes more subtly, when these factors or life views emerge.

While walking in a local park at the time of reflection on the project, I happened to throw a stone into an artificial lake in the grounds, noticing the concentric circles that resulted. I realised that the ripples may indeed be a suitable metaphor for demonstrating the complexities within family relationships, and thus I was able to do the initial model construct for the Ripplegram.

And so Ripplegrams were borne as a concept, that I further developed when working with the team.

Ripplegrams

For older people living out their gender diversity in later life, a world of possibilities may open. The opportunity to be your authentic self, to feel liberated and more confident, are changes that some older Trans and Gender Diverse (TGD) people have reported in this resource. However, this process of change in a family may also result in conflict, communication difficulties and other challenges. The Ripplegrams section, presented in this resource highlight the possible consequences for older TGD people and their families when a change like this happens in established family relationships. (Barrett, C. *et al* 2019:3)

Out of this creative process came the idea and the image of the 'Dreambreaker'.

So you say, 'Who or what is the Dreambreaker?'

Well, a Dreambreaker could be someone like, or similar to me. The Dreambreaker may be a societal outlier from among the approximately 11% of the Australian population that comprise my sisters and brothers and others of the LGBTIQA+ community living and loving in the general population. In so many cases, for reasons of safety, health, finances, or work, many of us either choose or are forced to live in the 'metaphorical closet'.

I would contend the following human traits that create the hurt, harm and wreckage in some families of the Dreambreakers are as simple or profound as the dreams created when the knowledge of conception first permeates the consciousness of the parent(s), or parent(s) to be! Parental dreams are borne of hope, wonder, fear and even 'ownership' of new life that has started within, and of course stirred by the inevitable hope of renewal of life and the passing on of the genetic core / code of the parents. But more than this, the birth parents start the dreaming for the future that the new life within promises, at one level, a daughter or son, or other, to comfort and care for us as we reach our later life phase.

GREEN POSITIVE IMPACT – DECISION MADE.

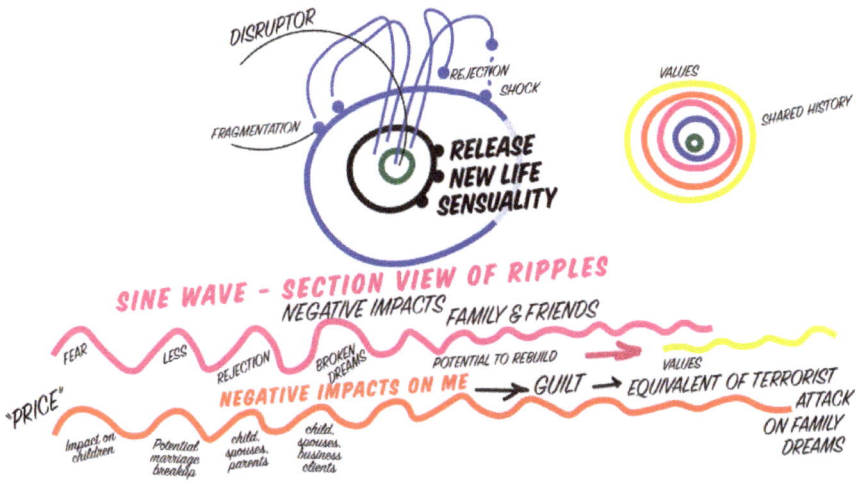

DISRUPTOR

REJECTION

SHOCK

VALUES

SHARED HISTORY

FRAGMENTATION

RELEASE
NEW LIFE
SENSUALITY

SINE WAVE – SECTION VIEW OF RIPPLES

NEGATIVE IMPACTS FAMILY & FRIENDS

FEAR LESS REJECTION BROKEN DREAMS POTENTIAL TO REBUILD VALUES

NEGATIVE IMPACTS ON ME → GUILT → EQUIVALENT OF TERRORIST ATTACK ON FAMILY DREAMS

"PRICE"

Impact on children Potential marriage breakup child. spouses. parents child. spouses. business clients

Pamela's example drawn from alicesgarage.net

However, I suggest that the dreams become more and more complex as, at first, the baby within shows signs of developing a healthy growth path towards eventual birthing.

But the birth of a healthy child is just the start of the lifelong empathic dreams of the couple involved or mother only, as is the case for some.

What should a 'Dreambreaker' expect or hope for? A societal model that respects others, that cares for other humans as for themselves, that is compassionate towards others. For we are humans too.

As the child develops, the dreams become more and more fleshed out, as the child grows through walking, running and schooling, the dream becomes more detailed and future-focused and eventually becomes infinitely more complex, more and more affirmed through a healthy growth cycle.

Eventually I believe that these life expectations become so real that they become fixtures, welded to the success model of the parents, and a failure to achieve what may be lofty goals become a comment and failure point for the parent. Thus, when the Dreambreaker breaks the news of their 'extra normal' branch out from those defined, pre-ordained plans of the parent, it's a potential catastrophic failure that may be unsustainable for the parent so involved, to either try to support or understand the unique spiritual life outlook of their child.

The dreams are natural and expected, however in some they are as reliable as the fabled house built on a foundation of sand.

I would like to think further development of the Ripplegram / Dreambreaker modelling tool currently under development may be of use in clinical relationship counselling for a range of my sisters, brothers and others in the broad church of the Rainbow community.

The Dreambreaker is an original concept developed by Kathy Mansfield.

*

Alice's Garage - https://alicesgarage.net/
The Kinfolk Project - https://alicesgarage.net/kinfolk/

Barrett, C; Mansfield, K; Bradshaw, K; Paynter, T and Conning, S. *RippleGrams. A resource to support older Trans and Gender Diverse people and their families*, Melbourne, Australia (2019).
https://alicesgarage.net/wp-content/uploads/RippleGramResourceHere.pdf

Kelly 4 Shannon 4eva More
G. JAE CURMI

It's funny, you don't realise how bad the things you live with every day are 'til you leave. I think I was lucky though – living on the edge of town instead of being locked up in the middle. Dad raised me the best he could. We had a flaky, weatherboard up the far end of Bent Street, past the no limit signs. I liked the name, 'cause it talked about me, without me having to say anything. Like a private joke. I liked it out there, mostly on my own. If it hadn't been for the school bus, I probably wouldn't have gone into town at all. It was too far to ride my pushy, especially in summer, but I promised Dad I'd go to school to keep welfare away.

Don't even know if the old house is still there, it was falling down even with us both in it. Dad never drank, but he wasn't there much either. He followed the shearing. I loved his lanolin soft hands. They made me smile when he let me run my fingers over them. I felt close to him then, for a little bit. They were so different from the rest of his hard, strong body. He never hit me with them much either, except if I didn't keep the house looking right or he'd come home and find me wearing his clothes. I couldn't help that, it's what I felt comfortable in. I especially loved putting his suit on. I liked how it looked, and how good it made me feel. He never wore it. Not since Mum left. But I don't like thinking about that too much. Neither of us did. So, it sat there heavy in the place where our love should be.

I hated school. I hated having to wear a uniform and being picked on for looking different, or not wearing a uniform and getting shit for wearing the wrong clothes. But I could take whatever they dished out to me, it's what they said about Mum that got me going. I was always copping shit for smashing someone when they tried to slag her off.

It wouldn't have been easy for her to leave. To leave him. To leave me. She was really brave, I reckon, coming all this way from some tiny little island in the Mediterranean. I looked up where Malta was in an atlas at school once. It's minuscule. Some maps don't even have it on them. But Mum used to tell me that Malta was actually five islands. Imagine that. One day I'm going to go there and see for myself. Mum was so proud of herself marrying an Aussie she chose instead of the Maltese boy her aunt tried matchmaking her with. She never knew then though, that Dad would take her all the way across the Great Divide to this barren hole of a place. Where cathead prickles lance through your thongs as easy as a piece of Wonderwhite bread. She hated them, and all the scary things that bit, like redbacks and snakes, and the born-and-bred locals who wouldn't accept her because she didn't look or talk the same as them.

Dad took Mum away from the only family she had in Australia, and away from the concrete safety of Sydney with its dance halls that she loved so much. I didn't know for a long time where she went after she left us. I'd get postcards now and then, but they were always stamped from different places so Dad couldn't track her down. He tried once or twice, but then gave it up.

But I'm not in Barraba anymore – not since Dad died while away shearing – got himself killed by a bloody randy ram, down Rangari way. It was hard, losing them both, but it also meant I was finally free. Free to leave. I'm not like Mum, though, can't stand cities. But Sydney was sweet for a while, to learn that I'm not the only one like this. That it's ok to be me.

I have got to talk about those times in Barraba though. Let folk know what it's like growing up and being in a place that's so far away from city technologies and influences that most people still don't even have computers or see much outside their own small lives and beliefs. And where being a square peg sux big time. So, I'll tell you the story of my leaving, which was hard. It's hard to go when you're leaving the only person who understands you behind.

'You can't go.'

'I know, but I'm going anyway.'

Kelly starts crying and I hold her close to my bound chest. I can feel a cathead prickle under my arse and try to brush it out without disturbing her too much. Her tears are starting to sog through my shirt. 'Come with me. Please.' My eyes are getting all hot and burny. Geez, I think I'm going to start bawlin' like a girl myself in a minute. 'You know I'll die if I have to stay here.'

I'm glad we're lying under our big old peppermint gum, carved with our love, at the back of the showgrounds. Its weeping branches sweep right down almost to the ground. Cocooning us. Hiding us. Maybe I'm not so different from Mum after all. She knew that staying here would kill her, and it will kill me too. Inside, if not outside, and probably both. And I'm still underage as far as welfare goes. Kelly hangs her head, avoiding my eye, 'You know I can't come. I can't leave Mum alone.' She looks up. 'Not with him.'

'I know.' My hands ball into useless fists. A huge roar goes up, and we both know someone's taken a bad fall or been gored if they're riding bulls. But there's no more shouts so I guess not too much damage was done.

I feel Kelly relax against me again. Her little brother's riding tonight and we'll have to go watch soon. He's hoping that riding the circuit will be his ticket out of here. But I don't want to move. I don't want to get up and face the world. I just want to lie here with Kelly in my arms and cathead prickles sticking in my arse forever. When I shut my eyes, still squeezing back the tears, I see rainbows of lights from the Spider ride spin across my eyelids and hear everyone squealing as it makes that big whoosh sound. I've got this big empty place inside me and I know it's only going to get bigger.

Please don't let this moment end … ever. But of course, it does. At least Kelly does it gently. She raises up on her elbow and looks me straight in the eye. It's hard to keep looking at her, but I do. I feel shamed that I'm leaving her. Abandoning her. So, I keep looking back at her, looking into her eyes. Both of us seeing into the depths of each other's souls. Connecting real deep. Deeper than sex even. She's the only person I've ever done this with, been this intimate, and it's breaking my heart all over again. This time I really do cry. Blubbering away like a little bub. And it's Kelly holding me. Stroking me.

'I love you, Shannon.' Her breath's a whisper in my ear. I can't say nothing. Just sob like the Split Rock Dam's been ruptured. As if I'm some stupid little kid who doesn't know any better. When I finally snivel myself dry, Kelly rolls on top of me and I really do have to get that cathead prickle out. She laughs at me wincing and flailing, but she doesn't get off me, just lies there chuckling low and deep in her throat. I finally get it out and even though I thought I was too heartbroke to want sex, Kelly starts slowly, rhythmically, ever so gently grinding against my body. Her fingers entwine mine and pin them to the ground above my head and another bloody cathead prickle digs in, but I'm past being able to even feel it now. I'm just looking at her. Feeling her. Loving her. Watching that slow sexy smile that always melts me, turn into something more.

Then another roar goes up and I feel Kelly tense, worried for her brother. The spell just broke and we both know it. Kelly gives me a gentle kiss on the mouth, and I pull her back as she goes to get up. I want the magic to come back, but it's gone so I don't struggle when she pulls me to my feet.

I try to keep us to the shadows as we head back towards the show. Out of the lights, and noise and dust. But Kelly takes my hand and walks into the glare of the lights, proud and smiling, and just daring anyone to say something. It makes me feel like I'm worth something, just to be with her. I stand up tall and walk next to her. For a while, I can even ignore all the looks and the snide whispered remarks.

'Bull-dyke!'

'Lezbo'

'Wog-slut!'

I can feel my fingers balling into fists again and my lip curling and I'm tempted to turn and punch out whoever makes the next sound. But Kelly's just walking like she can't hear nothing, and she looks at me smiling with that wicked grin she gets. She pulls me close, so our arms are round each other and suddenly that empty place inside me is filled with her warmth. I don't give a shit about what anyone says. It's our last night together and nothing's going to spoil it. I'm at the annual show with my girl and I'm going to win her that big stuffed unicorn she wants so bad from the shooting gallery, so she's got something to hold onto when I'm gone. Something to remember me by. To keep our hope and our love alive 'til I come back for her like I promised. A proper man.

*

Sydney's alright, but I miss Kelly real bad. I've tried ringing, but her old man always answers and bullshits she isn't there. Maybe things will change when my voice does.

I'm staying at Twenty10 refuge. The other kids, and workers too, are pretty cool. But I'm still looking over my shoulder, can't seem to break that old Barraba habit. Hard to believe I'm safe or that I'm not the only one like this. Mostly they're gay and been kicked out of home. City kids in designer label haircuts and the latest smartphones, woosing on about bindi-eyes. I should've brought some catheads with me and stuck them in their sheets. Then they'd know what a prickle is. The workers gave me a phone, too, with credit even, but Kelly doesn't get reception.

There's a few here like me. Mostly m2f, but there's another f2m, and one of the workers, too. I even know there's a name for people like me who didn't get born in the right body. I'm trans. Female-to-male. Braden says I don't have to change anything to be a transman. He hasn't. But I do. I don't want anyone thinking I'm a girl anymore. Kelly doesn't care that I'm short, but some here say you grow more on T. I hope so. Can't wait to start transitioning, for my body to show on the outside who I am inside. I thought it'd be easy. But there's all sorts of doctors you've got to see. All judging you. What if they say no? One worker said he'd come with me when I go. Maybe I should let him. But I've always done things on my own. Like my dad. I've never done anything this big before though. Jack's good to talk with, too. Knows what it's like for me, 'cause it was the same for him.

'You know there's some things you can't ever reverse, Shannon.'

'Yeah, I know.' I can't take my eyes off Jack's Adam's apple. One of the irreversible things I'm busting to have. I run my hand over my own smooth throat.

'That's all the doctors want to be sure of, eh? That you won't regret the confirmation treatments. That they're doing the right thing by you.' Jack's fingers rasp through the dark stubble on his chin and I wonder about his own decision.

'Was it hard for you?'

'Nope. I always knew. And I've never regretted my decision. It never felt like a *choice*.' Jack's smile is a sunburst. My own grin splits wide-open, 'cause that's just how I feel. 'Mind you, I could've done without this!' He rubs the bald spot on his head and we both laugh.

'Did you're voice break and go all squeaky? Did all the zits come back? How was it, watching your body change?' Yep, the Split Rock dam just burst, flooding him to near drowning, with all my bottled-up questions.

'Whoa! Slow down, brother.' He holds up his hands in mock defence.

Brother. Cool! He just called me brother.

'The hardest part was my parents. Losing the daughter they never-really-had and gaining a second son. But, they're okay now. Accepting of me and whoever I bring home.'

Wow. I can't imagine that. Fantasy. *Barraba Gazette* headlines: 'Trans man, Shannon Saunders, Welcomed Home with Open Arms'. More like, 'Take up Arms, Open Fire!' But I *will* go back. To get Kelly. I promised. And nothing's changed there, except me, I guess. I can't let myself think that far ahead, though, or I won't be able to bear staying away. Doing what I need to do.

Its nine months now since I started T. I stroke my happy trail, knowing why they call it that, 'cause that's how I feel most of the time. Walking 'round with this silly idiot grin on my bum-fluff face. The doctors were full-on, but Jack's support helped heaps. I love how I've muscled up, working out. No-one sees me as anything but male anymore and I feel so comfortable in my skin. I have a job detailing cars and I've nearly saved enough for top surgery. Got my Ps too. I hope the yard will sell me one cheap when I'm ready to go.

Missing Kelly is a blunt fulltime ache these days. It's been hard with no contact. Can't even write 'cause it won't get past her old man. I wish I could teleport there and back again. Just to see her. Touch her. Tell her I think of her all the time. That it won't be long 'til I come for her. It better be soon, 'cause even my memory of Kelly is getting blurry. Wish I had a photo. But maybe the ache would wake into something worse.

'Ready mate?' Jack's at my door.

'Hang on.' I've been saying goodbye to my boobs in the mirror. I actually feel a bit sad. Dunno why, 'cause this is the day I've been dreaming of. There's no understanding feelings sometimes. I tug on my binder, push my boobs into place, then throw on my T-shirt and jeans. I stand sideways, running my hands down the smooth line of my chest. After today, it'll be legit. No more binding. Ever.

'Ready.' My voice is deeper than Jack's. So far, so good with my head hair, too. I'm not thinking about the actual surgery though, 'cause I felt queasy just watching a doco on it. Jack's frowning. Waiting for some cue from me.

'Let's do it!' I high five him and he grins.

It looks fucking awesome! I left work after top surgery. Though the boss gave me such a good deal on the wagon, I got inked as well. I love it, walking shirtless down the street, people sneaking a look at the tattoo. The phoenix's fiery wings spread right across my chest covering the scar. It's got its head nestled between my pecs but looking up. Fierce. Like it's got purpose with that strong upbeat of its wings, and its long blazing tail rising from the flames of my happy trail.

The only thing missing is Kelly. It's eighteen months, maybe, I've been away and I can't wait to see her. Can't wait for her to see me.

But now it's almost time to go, I keep putting it off. I'm a bit scared of looking at why though. What I might find if I look too close.

'Reckon it's time mate. We'd have moved you to a half-way house if you were staying in Sydney.' Jack's looking at me over his mug at the kitchen table. Not frowning, just looking. Telling me like it is. Chucking me out. I'm just glad there's no-one else around to see it.

'Yep. Well, I'll get goin' then.' The words come out stiff and gruff, but honestly, I feel ready to blubber. I push off the table. Turn to go. Jack reaches out, stopping me with a hand on my arm.

'I don't mean now, Shannon. It's just time to think about it.'

'Good a time as any.' I hear my voice snapping but can't help it. I clench my jaw to fight down bile, and feelings and hold them down. This is something I'm used to. Good at. I pull my arm out of his grip.

'Shannon. Wait. What's coming is the hardest bit. I know. I went through it too. Going back to the people who knew me most, before I transitioned.' He's looking at me, sympathy brimming in his eyes, and it just about undoes me.

'What if Kelly doesn't recognise me? Or like me anymore … like this?' My voice is so whispery I don't know if Jack can hear it. I'm talking to myself as much as him. There's stupid snail-trails on my face, drips catching in my stubble. I give them a swipe, in a pretending-they're-not-there kind of way.

'Well, you'll never know, if you never go … you don't have to though. There's room in our halfway house if you want to stay. You'd be welcome.' Jack tugs on his goatee. 'If you want, we can find a place for both of you …' I shake my head. I couldn't imagine ever wanting to come back to a city, but it's nice Jack's offering. Knowing there's somewhere to come back to if things don't work out makes it seem a bit less scary. I'm even feeling excited again to see Kelly. A bit sad, too. Jack's been the best support anyone's ever been, except for Kelly.

'Stay in touch, bro. If you want. Let me know how things go. And ring me on that phone if you just want to talk, or whatever.' We both stand up and do that awkward man-hug thing. And then, fuck it, I pull him close and give him a proper hug.

'I'll miss you, man.' I can feel myself blushing, but it's all good. It's alright for a man to show he cares.

I feel joy rising up in me, just like that phoenix on my chest. Tamworth. Shit. Just a couple more hours. I'm nearly home. Whatever that is. The only thing 'home' about Barraba is Kelly. Home is where the heart is, I guess. Like that old song. Patsy, the wagon, hasn't missed a beat. She's just purring along the highways, slick as. I'm going to make myself eat something at the Golden Guitar even though I'm not hungry. Me and Kelly used to come here sometimes, 'cause she loved country music. People used to recognise us too. So, I'm testing it out. To see if I pass. See if they still know me.

There's this dude behind the counter. Tim on his badge. He always used to curl his lip when he served us. I went up to him especially. But he's not even batting an eyelid. Just gave me a ticket, took my money and said, 'thanks, mate.'

Sweet!

I'm on Fossickers Way and that burger's sitting like a lump of asbestos out of Woodsreef mine. I'm so nervous I think I'll heave it. I've got a galaxy of plans. Just can't decide on which one. And all the time, niggling away, there's this little voice telling me Kelly isn't going to like what she sees.

Yep, I admit it. I'm gutless. I drove straight through town, out the other side and up to the lookout. I guess I hoped Kelly might be walking down Queen Street. But she wasn't. Here at the lookout, I can see the whole town. There's the bowlo, and I figure out Kelly's place from there. Now I'm here, I'm aching so deep. I just got to see her. I'm watching her front yard, hoping for a glimpse, but there's only her old man forking up catheads. He cares more about his bloody lawn than Kelly or her mum. School's not even out for a couple of hours. Time to shower and change. Work out what to do.

I call by my old house first, on Bent Street. Looks the same as when I left, except for the guttering hanging off, more smashed windows and some fading graffiti: GO HOME WOG DYKE. And the mailbox spewing junk. Stuck to the back of one is a water-damaged postcard from mum. A canefield lit up at night. Mackay. No wonder I couldn't find her in Sydney. Not that I tried really. Went to La Valette once, a Maltese social club out at Blacktown, but chickened out at the door.

I poke through the junk-mail again, hoping for a note from Kelly. Nope. Can't quite make myself go inside. Too many ghosts.

I feel like a stalker. Sitting a hundred yards from the top gate.

Then my heart's flapjacking all over the place 'cause there she is. My mouth's gone dry and I need to pee. Bad. I can hardly breathe she looks so good. I'm watching through my rear-view. She comes closer and I see she don't look so good after all. Got a hangdog look about her I've never seen before. Something's wrong. Her eyes are all puffy and there's fresh bruises on her arm. Is her old man beating on her as well as her mum? I'll fix him, the prick. She's scuffing past and I know I've got to say something.

'Kelly.' My voice comes out squeaky. Too quiet to hear. 'Kelly!' That's better. She looks, but through me and keeps walking, faster. I start up Patsy and crawl along beside her. Now I totally am a stalker. 'Kelly. It's me. Shannon.' This time she looks right at me. Squinting. Her mouth like a big O as she recognises me. 'Get in.' I push open the passenger door. She looks around then gets in. I head for the showgrounds. For our tree. Kelly still hasn't said anything. Just sits there staring at me. I pull up. As soon as I've cut Patsy's motor, Kelly starts whacking me. I hold my arms up over my face, feeling them bruise. I'm so surprised, there's no pain.

'You bastard. You fuckin' bastard!' There's rivers coursing down her face and snot dribbling. Her yells echo 'round Patsy as hard as her fists. 'You PROMISED! You promised you'd COME BACK for me.' At least she's stopped hitting me now. 'I waited. I WAITED and WAITED!' She's hitting me again. I sit there covering my head, waiting for the flood of anger to pass. This isn't quite the fantasy I had for our reunion. But I guess she has a point. So, I just listen and take it 'til she's done.

'Where were you? You didn't ring. Or write. I thought you loved me …' She's kind of folding in on herself. Her voice fading to a whimper. Punching herself instead of me. I grab her wrists, holding them. Not hard. Just enough so she doesn't hurt herself. I see she's been cutting again.

'I did try. I rang. But your old-man …' we both know I could've tried harder. 'I'm here now. I came back. Just like I promised. For you, Kelly. And your mum. We can all get out of here together.' It's like coaxing a feral kitten. She still has that look like I've betrayed her. But also like she wants to believe me. Hope flutters. Then her face hardens and new tears brim. I watch them, moving in slow motion. They linger on her chin then fall, one-by-one.

'It's too late, Shannon.' She hangs her head. Pulls her wrists from my hands.

'Nah. It's not.' I try to sound light but a black hole opens, sucking.

'Yes. It. Is.' Kelly thrusts her hand in my face so I can't miss it. A ring. A fucking engagement ring. I'm breaking up, nearing the epicentre. Frozen on some fucking event horizon.

'No. NO. NO!' I hear words booming round Patsy. Realise they're mine. 'No.' I thump the door open. Need air. Stumble away. Can barely see. I throw myself on the ground straight into a patch of fucking catheads. Well, at least I can still feel. Looking up I see I'm under our tree. There it is. Kelly 4 Shannon 4eva carved in a big love heart. The arrow pierces mine. I start heaving huge pathetic man sobs no-one ever hears in public. I pull out my penknife and start stabbing it. Bark flying. Flaying it like Kelly's words just done to me. Then I stop. 'Cause if I kill it, it'll be like our love never was. Was never real. And it was. It was the most real thing I ever felt. Kelly's right. I should've made more effort. Not given up ringing so easy. But why didn't she wait? Just a little longer. But … what if it'd been me waiting? Reckon I might have given up too.

Kelly's arms slip around my waist. Her warmth against my back. I want to hang on to my anger, but I never can with Kelly. I drop the knife and let her turn me. My traitor heart snap–thaws.

'I thought you'd forgotten me. Didn't want me anymore. Thought you'd started a new life in the big smoke. Found someone else.' Kelly eyeballs me, wanting to know if it's true. Sees it's not. Drops her gaze. 'How could I know, Shannon, when I never heard from you? How?' She looks at me hard again. 'You don't know what it's like. Dad's beatin' mum so bad I think he's going to kill her. When Dennis Hagan asked me out… '

'Hagan! Dennis Hagan's the biggest lout out. Why would you date that fuckin' bovine?' I push off Kelly's hands. 'That prick's the worst for slagging me off, too.'

Kelly reaches out, but I back away. 'Because he is a big tough shit. And I thought it might make dad think twice about beatin' up mum. I was wrong.' She looks fragile and shamefaced. I realise those bruises aren't from her old man at all.

'Hagan did this to you?' I'm ready to tear off and punch his face into compost. Kelly grabs me.

'Shannon. No. Shannon!' I turn back. See the fear in her eyes. For me. For what might happen to us both. To us all. 'There's got to be a better way.' She's holding my heart in her fist.

'Kelly. I love you. I've never stopped lovin' you. You were all I ever thought about. Every day. Every night. I did this for me, but for us too. So we can be a normal couple.' She looks so beautiful. Tears and snot, bags, bruises and all. She's my only heart's desire. My lips are on fire, I want her so much. But I'm not going to take advantage of her. 'I'm sorry I didn't come back sooner. I didn't know it had gotten so bad for you. I'd have come sooner if I could.' Bit of a lie.

'I've missed you so much, babe.' She pulls me to her, strips off my jacket and we lie on it to take the edge off the catheads. Lying there, holding each other, I feel all the hurt and abandonment and barriers leeching away. It's so right she's back in my arms. Nothing separating us. Fuzzy warm. I doze.

I wake startled. Something crawling through my stubble. I slap at it. It's a hand. Kelly's hand. Not a dream. She's actually here. Looking at me in that cheeky way I remember. Eyes dancing. Fingers straying.

'You're back. I got my man back.' Kelly's fingers unbutton my flannie. She giggles seeing my chest hair. Curls her fingers through it. Tickling me. Then gasps and rips my shirt open to look at the phoenix. All of it. And more.

'I gotta go. We're all goin' up the bowlo for Chinese. Dennis is comin' round at seven.'

My teeth grind when she says that. But I can cope now I know it's all alright. And we got a plan. They'll go out for dinner. Kelly will go to the loo when her mum does. They've already been talking of taking off, so it won't be a surprise. Later, Kelly will have a headache and get rid of Hagan. Then, when Kelly's dad is in a grog-induced coma, they'll sneak out the back. Easy-peasy. I'll be parked a street over. Lots of vacant blocks there, so no-one will see me. They wouldn't know me anyway.

I've been waiting so long, I'm nodding off. But what if something's wrong? What if Kelly changes her mind? Or her mum won't leave him. Thanks, brain. I'm wide awake now. Start chewing my nails. Wish I could put the radio on and distract myself. Another half-hour. Shit. What if they don't come? I'm chewing on the quick now.

Whispers. Loud in the night. I strain into the darkness. Glad the moon's behind cloud. They're here! I jump out of the car and fling open the doors. Kelly and her mum come running, giggling like you do when you're scared shitless and being brave at the same time. Patsy purrs to life. We hit the highway, up to the Gwydir then head towards them canefields in Mackay. *Back in Baby's Arms* courting us on the radio and Kelly's stuffed unicorn in pride of place on the dash. In the rear-view, Kelly's mum looks happier and younger than she has in years. She's got this big smile on her face, even with tears runnelling through her pancake. I think she's ok with it all. She squeezes my shoulder and sticks her head out the window catching the breeze. I look at Kelly and she's beaming back at me. I put my arm around the most gorgeous woman in the universe and she snuggles close. Sure, things won't be easy, I know, but right now, I reckon I must be the happiest man alive.

The first part of this story was published in *TEXT* Special Issue 32: 'Why YA?: Researching, writing and publishing Young Adult fiction in Australia'. eds. Jessica Seymour and Denise Beckton, (2015). The second part of this story was a presented paper at the 20th Annual AAWP Conference in 2015, 'Writing the Ghost Train'.

G. Jae Curmi has an intersectional, trans* identity and is currently a PhD candidate at Southern Cross University. Jae uses they/them pronouns and their research interests lie in documenting the gender affirmation experiences of trans* and gender diverse people in regional, rural and remote environments in Australia. Jae has recently left the Northern Rivers in NSW which has pretty awesome support systems for the highest population of LGBTIQ+ people outside the urban areas of Australia and moved to the Fleurieu Peninsula in South Australia, which has the highest population of pipis in Australia. The things you do for love.

image: Jamie James

Cassy

she her

Gender transition helped me to unlock a wellspring of joy that I've always yearned for …

Chains
NOAH SILVEREYE

The ship rocks from side to side, near hypnotic in its movements. The gentle current flows beneath it. People on board bustle about, chattering to one another. They go about their busy lives, their chains a constant clatter and cling as they live amidst themselves.

One person leans against the railing, taking in the sight of the depths below. Eyes squinting, they see a collection of cutters of all shapes and sizes, spread across the ocean floor as far as the eye can see.

This person fiddles idly with their own chain, the length of it a heavy weight connected to an unlockable clasp on their ankle.

Absentmindedly, they wonder what it would be like, a life without this chain weighing them down, yet tethering them to this giant ship named *Heteronormative* all the same.

They wonder what it would be like to simply dive down into those clear depths. To be able to break away from these chains that scream *Gender Gender Gender*, over and over again. It is impossible to speak out against those who insist otherwise, when the evidence is constantly attached to their leg like a leech attaches itself to skin.

The water is deep, far deeper than it appears with it's crystal clear serenity. In those depths, at the furthest point away from oxygen, of life and breath, therein lies many pairs of bolt cutters, scattered along the ocean floor.

Yet despite the risks, the person dives headfirst into the icy waters- for what else would the waters of this chilling world be but icy?

There are startled cries above them, from the ship they call home. Pleas and demands that they return. Still they dive deeper and deeper.

Each cry for them to come back tugs on the chain, each plea yanking at their desperately kicking legs. Still they proceed, through the salt in their eyes and the burn in their lungs that has them regretting not taking a deep breath. The promise of *their their their* becomes a chant in their head.

Images of their friends and fellow queers flash through their mind, of the acceptance and compassion those people without chains show. The solidarity and the confirmation that they are not alone fills their lungs with air, their legs with the strength to continue downwards. Slowly, with the salt of the ocean water, the chains that bind them begin to rust away.

They dive deeper and deeper into the depths. Each desperate, determined stroke of their arms and kick of their legs propelling them further and further downwards.

Soon they have swum so far below that their air is gone, just as the light of the sun high above is shrouded by darkness. Still they continue, fuelled by the love and compassion of their community, of the freedom they will gain once they obtain their bolt cutters.

The persistent tugging of their chain- their crew above desperately trying to bring them back-only fuels them further. Eventually, long after the nerves in their limbs have begun to scream in pain, after their vision has begun to fade, they are able to grasp their bolt cutters in shaky hands.

With renewed strength and speed, they twirl around and yank on their own chain, pulling on the rusted metal links until they are able to grasp them in one hand.

However, it isn't enough to simply hold it, and so in a move that desperately defies the laws of the ocean, they twist just enough to bring their teeth around the metal, gritting down on it.

Water floods through their parted lips, their lungs withering in fear at the oncoming flood. But the laws do not apply to them any longer, and so with strength once more renewed, they grasp the cutters in their two free hands. With one swift motion they snap the cutters clean through the links of the chain that has bound them all their life.

With the resounding SNAP! of the chains, heard even in the sound muffling waters, strength returns to their body, just as the need for air does. Adrenaline fills them and, quick as anything, they swim upwards. Desperation fills their lungs now far more than ever before.

Before, when despite their hopes they were still bound by chains. Now they are as free as the ocean of which they desperately fight, seeking out the makeshift grounding of the ship above.

They breach the surface, panting and gulping in lungfuls of precious air as the sun shines down on them, blindingly bright in comparison to the ocean's depths. They take a moment to appreciate it all, arms treading the water sluggishly.

Someone yanks them out of the water, harsh and scared tones surrounding them. Their crewmates heft them up, forcing them onto shaky legs as the masses of *Heteronormative* try desperately to reattach the chains.

There are a few that watch on in the distance, some simply watching the events play out incuriosity. Others with small smiles and a sense of kinsmanship, of *Pride*.

With those people watching on, the heavy weight of their chains no longer screaming other's ideals, they find the courage to say what they have longed to say for a very long time; 'My identity, once hidden behind chains and clasp, is something I shall no longer hide. And that, my fellow people, fills me deep with Pride.'

Chains was first read at Adelaide Feast in November 2020. Noah, they/them and transmasc, is currently studying recordkeeping, and story writing for fun on the side.

Weed Farm
CAT COTSELL

The first time I fell in love was bad. Not soap opera bad. Not the clearly labelled kind. It was the kind of bad that spawns from total emotional illiteracy. I'm standing in the shadowed corner of someone else's memories.

Being long past the processing stage I don't even want to think about it. It was ten years ago. All the same, it's not enough to feel embarrassed at certain recollections. You can't spank yourself with a bread knife and call that self-dissection.

I do call it love, what I felt, but I don't think it was recognisable as being that. Love, like art, can't be easily defined except to say there are different kinds, and whether they are good or bad depends on who you ask. Love isn't jealousy, anger, unconditional loyalty, or the relinquishing of one's identity, but it can be credited and framed with those things. What I felt was neurotic and greedy and clinging, like a grotesque child in a gothic horror novel, stunted because it wasn't ready to be born and had developed under toxic conditions.

I have to be melodramatic here because first love is a theatrical experience, and the only way to convey it truthfully is through adequately theatrical language.

The rough timeline looks tame. I had an intense crush on a fellow student and, following a friend's aggressive encouragement, told him. We dated for just over a month and then he dumped me. I was heartbroken and didn't get over it for half the year. I know because I kept a diary.

There was no physical violence, no assault, no lying or stalking or manipulating or clear and obvious abuse. It was a month in the lives of two teenagers. We were eighteen, old enough to think ourselves mature, young enough for inexperience, both mentally unready for the reality of hurting each other. I say 'each other'. I hurt him by how I acted on my feelings for him. He hurt me by not feeling for me and not pretending to. His hurt and mine were different teachers and taught different lessons.

In my diary, interspersed with seemingly self-aware sentences like I have to swallow the large, prickly reality that you are none of my business and my feelings aren't your problem and I expected too much without realising I was expecting anything, there are glaring gaps in empathy. Patches of words stretch thin and become transparent over the bulging self-pity beneath. I was entitled to him, and he had wronged me by taking himself away.

It wasn't my first relationship, but it was the first one I wanted to be in. I wanted like a snake wants out of its old skin, and around that want crystallised a feeling of ownership, although I wouldn't have called it that. I would have called it love.

At this stage I was out as bi to my friends. I did not know anything about myself other than that. I did not know I had inherited a pathological model of love from a broken family, I did not know I had a chemical imbalance in my brain, I did not know I was nonbinary. I include this last to give it emphasis. Gender trauma is not responsible for my conscious behaviour. I have other traumas that would make more convincing scapegoats. Social justice 101: recognition is not the same as action. Action begins with reaching into your own brain, feeling out the roots of the weed, and loosening its grip so you can pull it out completely and keep it from re-establishing. My crack in the pavement was a combination of pain, vulnerability, and ignorance. The fertiliser was love. The weed was me becoming his 'girlfriend'.

In that love there was a tangle of envy that I did not know how to parse. I liked my boyfriend's hands and knuckles and I liked it when he let me hold them, but those two likings were unalike. I liked his height, had always hated being short. I liked his jawline, liked how turning my head a certain way made my jawline more angular. I liked his eyebrows. I liked how dark and thick my own eyebrows were. I liked his short hair. I liked keeping mine short. I liked how his torso descended in a straight line down his hips, and I liked how my brother's hand-me-downs hid my hips.

Someone who has never experienced gender dysphoria might read vanity into that, but I never liked the way I looked. The dislike felt arbitrary at the time. I liked my freckles, my glasses, my dark hair, my hazel eyes, but I didn't like how I looked. I had never met anyone that disliked their entire femininity for reasons pure and integral. I thought only sexists disliked femininity, or felt abstract shame over it. I thought young women were taught to hate their appearance. And both of those things were true, so I did not think to replace them with something that felt truer.

Owning a boyfriend let me own masculinity without having to transpose myself. I could, through him, have a physical experience of masculinity, possess maleness, without having to undo the only frameworks I had for understanding myself.

Nobody had taught me about gender identity. I never made the connection that would clarify my protracted grief when he dumped me. I was not losing affection. He never gave me any in the first place. I had a shameless extrovert's power over a shy, awkward person, and between the two of us we barely had one person's worth of social skills. I did not know what I was losing except that something inside me was being torn out. As far as I knew, I was just a teenage girl walking home sobbing because I had lost the right to kiss the boy I loved.

How do you say 'I have lost the only window in my cell' to people that don't know you are in one? How does a wounded person make sense of their injurer's innocence when they can't comprehend the more obvious blows they've been dealt by others? All they can do is feel their way along in the dark, writing on the walls sentences like I can't see anything in you that wants to be with me and I do not know how to be close to someone and I can and will drag myself away from you.

Diaries, like love, like art, like gender, can be all sorts of things depending on who you ask. If you ask me, a diary is honest testimony and not intentionally so. It lets you see what you thought was happening, or how you chose to describe it. It lets you examine the carcass of your dead self.

I used to be imprisoned and I used to be a jailer. I used to be deeply unhappy, selfish and aware, oblivious, bitter, humiliated at myself for grieving a month-old relationship, relieved at how the exhausting intensity of my grief cast a numbness over everything else.

Love isn't something I understand any more than I did in 2009, and neither is gender, really. I've just learned that I am in a cell and how to open the window.

I fell in love recently. I have not told her and don't think I will. I value her friendship dearly and she is straight. She is also thoughtful, persistent, feminine, freckled, and tall.

We have a great capacity to hurt each other. We don't have to be dating to do it.

The more I check my brain for weeds, the more familiar I become with where the cracks in the pavement are. Sometimes I can fill in the cracks. Sometimes I need to pry up the concrete, turn the earth, and let weeds surface that I hadn't known were there so I can pull them out.

I hope, wherever he is, that he has pulled out the weeds I left in him.

Cat Cotsell reviews gender, self-expression, and all the other performances we put on. They are a creative generalist based in Canberra. Other writing and art can be found in volumes 3 and 4 of *Bent Street*, qommunicate's Hashtag Queer volume 2, Cicerone Journal's These Strange Outcrops, BMA Magazine, and FIVE:2:ONE.

COVID Exercise Bike
ERIN RILEY

Between March, when COVID-19 enveloped communities in fear, and August, as a second wave of infections had us retreating once more, I purchased three exercise bikes.

When the world was different, I had a rigid, routine life that involved the gym, the pool and the occasional pump class before work. My exercising had its own daily rhythm. I would take selfies in the bathroom mirror, put them on Instagram and inhale the dopamine hit that came from the flurry of likes, love heart eyes and fire emojis. Virtual poppers going straight to my head. The validation of the gender queer body.

My gym-going, while not really a secret, was one I kept guarded. I never spoke about how long or how often I was there. How significantly organised my life was around exercise. I didn't talk about how it functioned as a cheap way to regulate my feelings of dysphoria. Dysphoria around my body, my gender, and how they coexisted.

I didn't speak to the thoughts I had that if I didn't go, my body would transmogrify into something grotesque. I held close to my tiny chest shameful feelings that, intellectually and socially, I knew were unspeakable. The feelings that gave energy to the values I did not wish to hold – fatphobic, ableist ones that ran counter to the body-positive, woke queer I believed myself to be. While I didn't believe anyone else needed to fit narrowly-defined, socially-prescribed standards of beauty and attractiveness, I held an unreachable bar for myself.

Exercising made my body liveable. My gym-going, lap-swimming, the pump class – while they gave rhythm to my life was the container that held so much in.

I live opposite a swimming pool and a gym. Before lockdown, my social media feed teemed with information about how if Australia was going to flatten the curve, we needed to be socially-distancing. Staying away from places where people gathered together. Places like gyms and pools. Like many anxious people, I was infuriated by people's seeming wilful ignorance, their blatant disregard for the safety and health of others. Weeks before lockdown, I wrote exasperated posts on Facebook, encouraging friends to think critically, to change their behaviour. I spent an entire afternoon constructing an enormous cardboard sign and stuck it to the bedroom window in a desperate attempt to inspire community accountability:

Don't be dim and go to the gym. Save a mate and isolate!

I saw passers-by squinting up to read it. A man took a photo of it on his phone. I thought that perhaps my sign would become a viral sensation, encouraging people everywhere to get out of pools.

While all this was happening, I was deeply troubled by the collapse of my routine. I cancelled my gym membership and retreated into my apartment. I was angry but jealous of these people disappearing in and out of the gym, attending to their routines. I needed mine, too, but something much bigger was at stake. My dysphoria-maintenance routine had been short-circuited by a global pandemic.

It is interesting to think about it now, that it was the needs of others, and not my own mental health that inspired my premature retreat. A theme that has simmered in my life is that the needs and comfort of other people come first. My routine, unchanged in many years and, for as long unchallenged, was over in a day.

And so, I bought exercise bike number one.

When bike number one came, I realised it was a small toy disguised as a piece of fitness equipment. I had been fooled by an internet sale and, realising no rigorous exercise would be happening on its fragile frame, I dipped into my dwindling savings and purchased a name-brand spin bike. I hoped that by splurging I'd avoid similar disappointment.

As a younger person I held onto a warped notion of what my body looked like. I say warped because I had so little choice and few models for what was possible for a body to be. As someone coming of age pre-Internet, the idea that I had just two genders to choose from, in order to try and 'succeed' in the body I had been born and socialised into, didn't help me much with my body problems. I had a hard time meeting the standards of the gender the world had so effortlessly placed on me and wore it for decades like an ill-fitting shirt.

It is interesting that these narratives around crafting and maintaining the 'perfect' body permeate queer culture too in such invasive ways, even though so many of us often don't meet the normative ideas of gender or bodies circulating around us. Our bodies, to many, so far from perfect – out of line, illegible, other. I remember my mother's bitter disappointment so vividly when one night I arrived at my parents' house with a fresh fade. Her face visibly pained, her tone acrid and crushing, *why do you have to make yourself so unattractive?* To her, nothing was more unattractive than a feminine masculinity.

My distress around how much I was exercising, or the thoughts that I was failing to de-construct the powers I believed I was immune to, didn't leave much room for a more compassionate reading. There wasn't space to interrogate what else I had been trying to achieve, control and manage. Fatphobia and ableism defy gender lines and are deeply rooted in a society and culture that celebrates non-queer, non-trans, non-feminine bodies. I, like many people, wasn't immune to dangerous cultural messaging – of which certain themes stand out. Certain bodies hold currency.

Exercise bike number two arrived. Sturdy and sleek. I put on my grey bike shorts, took my spin class internet subscription into the garage and closed the electronic garage door. I pedalled a lot at 'racing resistance' and 'standing attack' in the dark to my new favourite spin class instructors Glen, Dee and Brent from LesMills on Demand. I started to hear the pulsating cover tracks in my head. My Pandemic Plan B.

Much of my exercising has been less about meeting certain standards placed upon bodies (though I think I have been held hostage by these dangerous myths for years) but about trying to transform it. It is a new realisation; one deeply rooted in long having felt uneasy in my skin. Of course, there is the enjoyable aspect of being fit and well, healthy and mobile, but for me, the shadow side of this was obsessive and clinical. As if, in going to the gym enough, being hard enough in my body, being buff, getting more buff, some of the feelings of dysphoria, the ones I did not wish to entertain, could be curtailed.

The gym and exercise *was* my gender affirmation. Somehow, in my head, it was a version of the medically-assisted transition I was yearning for but not willing to admit to wanting for myself. So, the daily ritual, much like taking hormones, was an aspect of affirming my gender every day. One I was hopeful was 'enough'. So much about the policing of my queer body via regimented exercise was about transforming my gender. A way of convincing myself that I was 'doing' something about it.

I had somehow conned myself into the belief that the gym would allow me to transition in the ways I wanted to, inside the gender assigned to me by others – as if by magic. As if in working out hard enough, I would be read by the world around me as the person I knew myself to be, who was not a woman and not a man and I could do this without distressing anyone – mostly my parents, who I knew might be most distressed of all. And so, for years I was bench-pressing into an idea of myself.

And then, mid mountain climb, the resistance knob of the second exercise bike stopped working. I was devastated.

After three weeks and forty-six email exchanges between Gym & Fitness, an internet gym-equipment provider, and myself later, exercise bike number three arrived.

I unpacked the new bike the day it arrived, one rainy cold wintry afternoon.

My neighbour Akira is ten years old and lives with her mum in the unit below. I see her in the stairwell some mornings when she is going to school. The last time I saw her I was on the second spin bike pedalling furiously and she caught me with the garage door open. I quickly stopped. *You're so fast and strong!* she said, which I found cute and encouraging. I got off and walked over to her. She had her bag packed and was going to a friend's house for her first ever sleep-over.

I recognised in Akira something I remember in myself as a small person – a desire to be noticed by adults. To please, to be seen, to be found interesting. She often wanders into the garage when she sees me in there. We talk about school, television shows, food we love. How I find it impressive that she can speak two languages while I have only one. She asked one of those innocent child questions only children can about age – asking who was the eldest of my housemate and I. Before I could answer, she candidly told me she thought I was *the young one.* I told her frankly that I was probably the same age as her mum and she point-blank would not have it.

As I was putting exercise bike number three together, Akira skipped into the garage. We pieced the bike together. I handed her the Allen key, we consulted the manual, she screwed bits into place and I moved out of her way so she could lie down and screw the pedals on.

As we were tinkering with the bike, I remembered the small version of myself. How meaningful it was when they were noticed, talked to as if they were special. I remember how my heart swelled. When we'd finished, Akira and I got up and dusted off our knees.

Are you a boy or a girl?, Akira asked, out of the blue as I was peeling lint from my tracksuit pants. *I'm a bit of both,* came my reply. *I thought that!* Akira said, enthusiastically.

I appreciated that her curiosity about my gender was something that came to her an hour into our bike-tinkering. That it wasn't so important. In the world, in which binary understandings of gender are still so pronounced, there seems to be this need for other people, mostly cisgender people, to decipher and categorise gender diverse people in order to understand or move to the topic of conversation. As if until they can clock us through the limited lenses culture affords them, the words coming out of our mouths are jibberish – made comprehensible only through the other person's skilful ability to box us into something knowable.

The replacement bike was repositioned in the back of the garage and Akira mounted her own small orange BMX. She put on her helmet. I'd seen her trying to learn to ride her new bike in the common area outside the unit block before, though I don't let her know. I don't tell her I have seen her straddling the seat with her tip-toes on the ground, periodically shrieking when she thinks she's about to fall off.

Watch me! she orders. I was ten years old when I learnt to ride a bike, I tell her. I watch her and I say some encouraging words and I stand there in my tracksuit pants and smile as she plays. She turns back to make sure I'm still watching. I'm the adult now and she is the small me, desperate to be seen. It is an easy gift and I value my newfound job, to remind her that she is special, important and clever.

I don't tell Akira about the time I was ten and had finally mastered my Malvern star with the flowery banana seat., when my

mum took me to the bike park and I rode around in my red
monochrome tracksuit and a group of boys shouted at me,
sarcastically, *nice bike*. I didn't tell her that I rode back to mum, full of
shame, put the bike down at her
feet and asked to go home. How I never once rode it again.

After a few brave pedal-strokes, Akira finds her pace and at the
last minute saves herself from toppling.

For a long time, internalised transphobia gripped me tightly, as did
my desperate need to demonstrate that women can look like me –
they can straddle the in-between and walk the edges of gender. My
desire to be a model for others outstripped my need to be honest
with myself about how I actually felt about being a woman in the
world. Even a butch one. It never felt like me. But the idea of
medically assisted transition to being read as a man in the world
wasn't me either, though I thought about it often.

I told myself that it was a gift to be a woman in the world. That I
had a big job to carry out. I told myself that I was 'comfortable'
being a woman and even if I wasn't, it was an important body to be
born into. There was much work to do in deconstructing ideas of
what women can be, I reminded myself. Despite the fact I felt uneasy
in my body for years, I repeated this story so often I believed it to be
true.

Thinking about transitioning medically, to find my place in the
middle, for a long time felt like I would be reneging on something I'd
promised the world, in all those years of self-denial. I worried it
would solidify homophobic and transphobic ideas in other people
that all butch women just want to be men. That it was misogynist of
me if I couldn't deconstruct the patriarchy that had conditioned me
into needing and wanting the masculinity that was just a construction
anyway. I told myself that focusing on the individual who was already
privileged enough was unimportant – there were greater injustices
that needed my attention. Transition, pronouns, making space for
new, re-fashioned and (re) affirming versions of ourselves was always
something for other people – but never something for me.

On reflection, my exercising was confining the possibility of what my
life could look like. I saw myself change with exercise but not in the
ways I wanted most. I didn't want to be seen as a man, but I was so
consistently distressed whenever I was referred to as a woman, as a

'lady'. It disturbed, so profoundly, the image I held of myself. So, while in my rational brain, I knew the gym would never afford me the moustache I wanted, the deeper voice, the hardened frame; features I could not manifest on the elliptical machine, I convinced myself that it was enough.

Like all people, we understand ourselves through a mediated world. One in which social and cultural shifts impact how we understand ourselves in relation to others. We are influenced and shaped by the representations around us. The physical and material reality of my life – for most of it, provided me so few options in which to see myself reflected back. I didn't see any genderqueer kids on television, in books or magazines. I didn't see many gay characters on the television either and when I did, that was mostly all I had. While gender may be a construction, how it has been crafted in the world influences how we understand ourselves in very real ways. So, while I have been a non-binary person for my entire life, this understanding was so far outside of my grasp, in both language and real-world possibility. It wasn't an option because I did not see it. I have never been a girl or a boy, a woman or a man – though for years tried to squeeze myself into one of them because it was the closest fit.

2020 has been a time of great shifts. I have begun to see myself as worthy. It has taken many years of therapy, but I have learnt to say no. No to things I don't wish to do, no to things that take away from what is important to me. No to things done out of obligation, to please others. I have learnt to love myself.

Doing things for other people, in my work as a social worker and in my personal life, was a constant theme. The idea of sticking to being a woman in the world was for other people. Not indulging the possibilities of affirming my gender, moving toward something authentic. That too, was for other people.

On Christmas Day 2019 I took testosterone for the first time. I began a new, daily ritual – gifting myself the small grace of affirming who I already am. In some respects, it was a move long overdue, a simmering desire held in place by an unchallenged ritual disrupted by a pandemic.

The unfolding comedy of the malfunctioning bikes and the entry of a small ten-year-old bike-tinkering messenger was the gift I didn't know I needed. A reminder of the deeper things that need more attention and care than just being contained. The time afforded by the pandemic gave me the space to think more about the function of exercise in my life. Underneath it, a deep knowledge was waiting for its time.

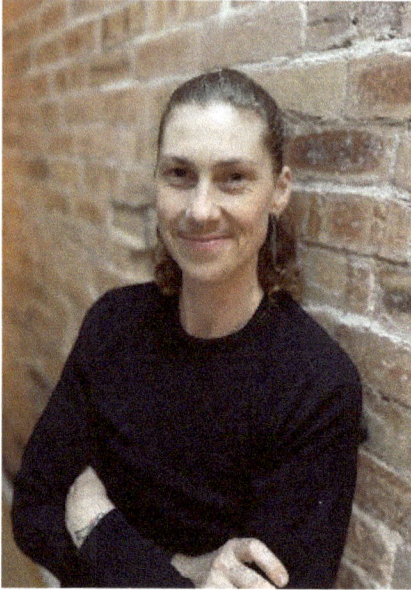

Erin Riley is a 36-year-old non-binary trans social worker from Sydney. They have worked in aged care for most of the last decade but now work as a palliative care social worker in the (in)justice system at Long Bay Prison. Erin enjoys reading, making breakfast and routines that rarely change.

In 2021 Erin received a Penguin Random House Australia Write It Fellowship to develop their creative non-fiction manuscript *Wrestling With Feelings*.

image: Jamie James

Indi

she her

I thrive from Life …

TRANSCENDE
TRANSITIONS
TRANSFIGUR
TRANSFORMA
TRANSLATIO
TRANSMISSIO
TRANSITORY
TRANSPORT
TRANSCONTI
TRANSPACIFI
TRANSATLAN
TRANSFIX
TRANSILLUM
TRANSLUCEN
TRANSPADAN
TRANSACTIO
TRANSVERSE
TRANSCEIVE
TRANSFIGUR
TRANSFORM
TRANSFUSE
TRANSIENT
TRANSISTOR

I call myself 'trans'
KAI ASH

I am in awe of the word *trans*. It connects me to words like *transcendence, transitions,* and *transfigurations.* Words like *transformation, translation* and *transmissions.*

I prefer it to the other word I could use – *transgender.*

Or, worse – *transsexual.*

Those words have been tainted in my mind. They have been so closely tied together with stories of pain and humiliation that I find it hard to unlink them.

When I speak the word 'transgender', I'm ten years old again, watching my current hero Jim Carrey prance across the screen in *Ace Ventura: Pet Detective* (1994). I reach the end and, without anything explicit being said, I learn that trans women are murderous and physically repulsive.

I'm a teenager again, watching crime show after crime show where the body on the slab is a trans woman's body and she has been battered and broken.

I'm an almost-adult sitting in my university lecture theatre watching *Boys Don't Cry* (1999). I flinch and cover my eyes and ears, trying to keep out this new lesson that it is not just trans women who are to be violated and killed, but trans men too. To be transgender is to be unwanted and reviled even by 'friends'.

I'm a real adult, walking through inner west Sydney with one of my closest friends and we're discussing sexuality. The conversation shuffles sideways into the subject of transness. He asks about my own gender and I make a flippant answer. I know my gender is more complicated than the next person's. I know others would call me genderqueer or gender nonconforming. But I don't yet feel that I need to call myself trans. I don't even realise that it's a real option. The only transgender people I'm aware of are either entertainers, prostitutes, or dead. I'm none of these things, so a 'cis woman' I remain. For now.

And then I am thirty. I am looking in the mirror and I see a face that is my own staring back at me. As ever, I am slightly surprised by its appearance. It never quite matches the form in my mind's eye and instead looks like a curious collage of my father, my mother, my aunts and my grandmothers. As I think through the genesis of each feature, I marvel at how they have all been rearranged to form *this* face and *this* body and that they are mine – or are they me? Am I the body? Or the mind within it?

These are questions I rarely grow tired of, but on this night, I don't take the time to truly marvel. Instead, I stare straight into my own hazel eyes – which are also my father's hazel eyes – and I wait for myself to acknowledge the obvious. I wait and I stare and, finally, when I can bear the silence no more, my mouth opens and I say to my mirror image:

'I am trans.'

And my mirror image stares back, relieved, and supremely unsurprised.

The lack of surprise is the dominant theme of my 'coming out' process. There is fear and worry, as my friends and family were raised on the same violent stories that I was, but very little surprise.

'That makes so much sense,' writes my cousin-in-law when he hears the news.

In Brisbane, my mother bumps into my primary school music teacher and, in the midst of their catch-up, mentions my transition. My old teacher is unruffled.

'That's what the kids used to say,' she says to my mother. '"Micci is a boygirl."'

Why did it take me until my thirties to call myself trans? Was I repressed? Was I in denial? Was I *not* trans before then?

They're all good questions, though I have few answers for you.

Two years ago – pre-trans-declaration – I was watching Hannah Gadsby's *Nanette* (2017) and there was a section that touched on transness. Hannah Gadsby described an interaction where she was told by a stranger that not only was she actually transgender but that she had a duty to the transgender community to be open about that fact. As Hannah Gadsby then told the audience, bemused and confused, 'that was new information to me.'

When I was watching the segment in 2018, I didn't even *hear* the word 'transgender.' I heard 'intersex.' For months afterwards – until I watched the show again – I thought Hannah Gadsby had been told by a perfect stranger that she was *intersex* and that she needed to be more open about it.

Was that inability to even hear the word 'transgender' a sign of repression? Or perhaps denial?

Maybe. It was certainly odd.

One thing I am sure of is that I didn't *feel* repressed. At least, no more repressed than I thought I should feel as a woman in this world, thanks to all the Lady Rules I'd learned over the years: *smile, agree, be quiet, stop taking up so much space, smile, don't wear that, don't burp, smile, don't fart, smile, be careful, smile, be wary, smile and shh!*

But it wasn't all bad. Much of it was good, even very good.

I grew up surrounded by admirable women. While I may not have felt a great deal of ownership over my feminine body, I did experience a bit of pride that, encased within it, I held a ticket to the Women Club.

At family gatherings, I could sit right in amongst the action without any awkwardness, while my brothers were relegated to the edges alongside my father, my uncles and male cousins. In my school and university classes, I could confidently speak on subjects like gender equality and sexism, secure in the knowledge that my female body gave me authority on the subject. No one would question *my* right to speak.

But, inside, I questioned it. I questioned my authority and my right to claim womanhood, because it always felt like something outside of me. It was the image in the mirror that always surprised me.

Many trans narratives suggest that I should hate my body, that it should distress me. And I understand the force behind that type of trans experience, I do, but it's not my story.

I have always been able to put aside my unease over my physique by drawing on the simple expedient of not thinking about it. I forget until I am confronted with a mirror, and then I'm surprised. Sometimes that surprise is unpleasant, but most often it's merely curious. How strange that I am within my body every moment of the day and yet I can never quite hold an image of it in my mind. How strange that I can feel my maleness in every cell and yet, the body in the mirror is quintessentially female-looking – when naked, at least.

When covered up, its presentation is far more ambiguous, accounting for a lifetime of '*sir, oh, sorry, I mean ma'am.*'

When I begin to call myself trans, a pressure disappears from my body. I had unknowingly been wearing womanhood like a corset, shaping my behaviour and interactions according to particular Lady Rules of my own devising, though inspired by the words and actions of those around me. I was becoming more and more constrained until I could hardly leave my flat for fear of bumping into a neighbour and them *seeing* me and my wrongness. I was trying so hard to be a proper woman, like all the women I love and admire, but it was hurting me because *I am not like them.*

And then the depression came.

Those dark times have left few traces in my mind. My brain rebelled against the melancholy and refused to form memories. I know that months were passing because I was given a new calendar for Christmas. And then another. Until, finally, I re-emerged after two missing years, knowing that things had to change. I had to make new decisions.

It was then that I discovered the word *trans.*

Trans is *translocation* and *transformation*. It is *transitory* and *transient* and *transversal.* It is not fixed or permanent or homogenous.

I look at myself in the mirror and I call myself trans.

And then I think, *what next?*

What came next was a long series of conversations with friends and family and colleagues. Then came the more official stuff: name change and information updates with companies and government agencies. Interspersed with all this was the shopping and the raiding of my male partner's closets for clothes that I had always preferred but had never been sure about wearing – another one of my Lady Rules, which required me to only wear the feminine cuts of shirts, pants and undies.

Some clothing I kept, because it was comfortable and I liked it and why would I throw out something that was perfectly serviceable? My partner declared my shoes had pink on them and should be abandoned immediately. I refused, saying that they would go once they carked it and not a moment earlier!

I can't remember the exact moment I discovered the word trans and learned that being trans was a real option. It came on so slowly. A story here, a story there, each one about characters who were trans and *happy*.

Most of these stories came to me through the medium of fanfiction – that crazy chaotic world where people take established characters out of their usual story lines and throw them into new narratives. I became obsessed with trans characters from the Harry Potter universe: a trans Hermione, a trans Lupin, a trans Snape, a trans Harry. Trans-male, trans-female, transitioning or already transitioned, it didn't matter, I read every word. What mattered is that these characters weren't constantly being spat at or raped or murdered. Instead, they were making friends, forming relationships and *getting on with their lives*.

Bit by bit, this new and exciting option was opening up around me.

In the quiet of the night and in the brightness of the day I was beginning to form an idea that maybe, just maybe, it was possible to be both trans *and* live a long and fulfilling life.

I am trans and I am happy. Happier than I was before, I mean. Life is never a state of constant joy but calling myself trans has increased my collection of happy moments and made the unhappy moments easier to bear.

Sometimes I'm asked if it has made anything harder, and my answer is always no. The fact is that I was never good at being a woman, no matter how many Lady Rules I developed and adhered to. Well before I transitioned, I was being harassed in women's toilets by people who believed I didn't belong there. I was routinely identified as lesbian, despite my male partner, which led to several awkward situations – not *bad* situations, just awkward ones. I was occasionally yelled at by people in passing cars, who must have assumed I was a gay male, judging by the slurs they hurled my way.

What I'm saying is that there has always been a disconnect between who I am and how I'm perceived, which means that there is very little in this trans space that is completely new to me. Except, of course, for how I feel standing within it. That belonging that enwraps me, that sense of rightness, like I don't have to question my right to be here – *that's* new. I don't remember feeling that before.

According to the usual trans narratives, this would be the part in the story when I toddle off to the GP to get a prescription for hormone replacement therapy and perhaps start the process for gender affirmation surgery. This would be the moment when I begin to reshape my body to make it more closely resemble the idea in my mind; the masculine form I wear in my dreams.

But there is a problem. I don't want to.

Well, I do and I don't.

The idea of getting rid of my breasts fills me with a giddy sense of excitement. What freedom! What joy! The idea of a lower voice gives me shivers of anticipation.

But the idea of doctors examining and prodding and cutting my breasts fills me with a cold fear. I have been here before. Between the ages of sixteen and twenty-two, lumps in my breasts led to years of doctor examinations and tests and pain and then finally relief when the breast cancer specialist announced her confidence that they were indeed benign fibroadenoma, colloquially known as *breast mice*.

What if I go ahead with the surgery – the cutting away of my burdensome breasts – and there are complications? What if I have to return to the doctors, to the surgeons, again and again? What if the scarring goes wrong and I'm left in pain every time the weather changes? Don't I already have too many scars beneath my clothes that hurt me in this way?

Hormones, too, scare me. I remember the breast cancer specialist warning me to remain vigilant, particularly if I go on the contraceptive pill or become pregnant. She said that, in the face of such changes to my hormone levels, my apparently benign breast mice may prove to be something far more malicious.

Wouldn't taking testosterone amount to the same thing? Wouldn't I be risking a return to all that pain and dread?

And then there's the issue of *how* I would introduce masculinising hormones into my body.

Needles? Every two weeks or three months for the *rest of my life*? Strongly scented gel or creams rubbed over my body *each and every day*? I don't even wear scented deodorant! My shampoo is a three-in-one product designed for children that only has the faintest whiff of artificial scent. And then there are the blood tests – every six months initially – to ensure that my hormone levels remain safe and steady.

Could I really do all that? Could I bear it?

I speak to a GP and speak to another. I discuss with my partner and draw up pros-and-cons lists.

I have this idea that I'm meant to medically transition. I'm trans, a trans-male, and that means I should be on hormones and getting, at the very least, top surgery. Everyone says so and every doctor I see seems to take it for granted that I want to. And I do, sort of, but the more I learn, the less attractive it all appears to me.

Then my partner and I separate and my world goes topsy turvy and I put all consideration of medical transition aside. Maybe I'll return to it one day. Or maybe I won't.

I remain a trans man with the physique of a woman. I have no dark hair on my cheeks, my voice tends to rise high when I'm stressed or enthusiastic and my body fat goes straight to my thighs and backside.

Sometimes I wonder if my refusal to medically transition makes me nonbinary as opposed to truly trans. But when I experiment with the idea in my head – mentally describing myself as 'they' and using a formal 'Mx' marker before my name – I always ultimately reject it. Nonbinary pronouns and descriptors fit me no better than the feminine pronouns and descriptors did. There is no sense of rightness, no frisson of joy, like there is with their masculine variations.

I know my choices can confuse people. Friends and family are sometimes surprised to see me as I still am because they have been taught to believe that *trans* means medical transition. But it really doesn't.

Trans is *transgressive*. It takes the usual rules – including my old Lady Rules and my newer Transgender Rules – and it subverts them. It goes beyond and between and outside of them.

I am trans and my existence transgresses the usual understanding of man and woman and, perhaps for some, even the usual understanding of transgender.

Calling myself trans frees me. It makes it easier to leave my flat and to present myself to the world.

It is the best option available for me, and it became an option thanks to the myriad of trans lives being lived by others. Like great scientists, inventors and artists of the past, these people – who have called themselves transsexual and transgender and genderqueer and nonbinary – were able to conceive of a way of living that most people would have deemed impossible. They dared to transgress and, in doing so, opened up a new way for us to live full and rich lives.

The path they laid down is still rough, with several obstacles along the way, but it's there and with each set of footprints, it becomes smoother and firmer as well as more varied – because, naturally, it wouldn't be a *trans* path if it didn't have a multiplicity of detours, tunnels, staircases and divergence points sprouting higgledy-piggledy along the way.

Today I'm walking the trans man path without the aid of hormones or surgery. Tomorrow I may make a different decision and skip over to another branch of this winding way. Or maybe I won't. I'll still be trans all the same.

Kai is a trans autistic writer with an interest in gender and neurodiversity. Kai recently moved back to Brisbane after two years in Melbourne, where Kai was shortlisted for the Lord Mayor's Creative Writing Awards 2020.

Bittersweet
KIN FRANCIS

Dear lover,

I met you when I was the person who came across like an unnecessary apology and seemed to know all the ways to exit a room.

Do you remember when we met at my then-boyfriend's place around Halloween? I was wearing a dull-brown leather vest and a cowboy hat, with a red handkerchief around my neck. It might have been the first time I ever went out with my stomach showing.

You were with your then-boyfriend too, and your eyes and mine met for just those few extra moments long enough that I knew we'd make out at the club.

When we kissed again months later, laying down together in Peel Street park, we started to discover our love right before Christmas.

In grey, wet weather in February, all the queers still dressed up in our colours and partied at Gaytimes. You and I danced to Landslide by Fleetwood Mac. We grinned at each other and I swear the sun was out even though it was raining.

When it was time for me to leave for London, I ignored the feeling of making a wrong decision. I often pushed myself into work to avoid the restlessness of not knowing what I wanted outside of routine. We cried together in your car. It was the last time I'd see you for two months. Later, you sent me a video of you singing a song you wrote for me. I listened in bed and then again at the airport and then again while waiting to desperately return home after a week to escape the pandemic in London.

Not seeing anyone for fourteen days in self-isolation while knowing how badly we wanted to meet was painful but also extremely hot. It was easier thinking about you than facing the existential crisis of no longer being able to work and not knowing who I was anymore.

Every time our bodies pressed together like an envelope, I began to realise how many stories I had never shared. I needed someone willing to listen. Throughout my life it often felt like there was a vast distance between me and everyone else. How do I begin telling someone everything that I am?

We had our private discos with your flashing lights and your curated playlists. When we listened to Caroline Polachek and I cried, you told me that Pang was my album.

Somewhere along the line of being in love with you, going to therapy, trying medications, spending less time writing emails, I started to make choices that would bring me joy. We were teaching each other that joy is a choice. And one day I chose to be clear that I was non-binary.

Throughout lockdown I bought dresses and skirts and heels and discovered gender euphoria. When I would read trans experiences online I could never quite see myself in these moments. Then suddenly, they were all happening to me.

Wearing a dress and heels out in public for the first time felt like returning home. I was with you, at Rainbow House on Smith Street. And though we're no longer together I am thinking about these memories and all the moments before that add up to the person I am now.

When I studied writing I thought I would write more. I was learning so much, and while it felt like I finally understood how to write, I could no longer write without editing. I would stop myself again and again. Before I could finish a sentence, I would change it three times.

I think loving you is the antithesis of this. Loving without editing. I've learned so much now about how to love and I've done so much work to love myself. This writing I'm sharing is unedited, mostly.

Do you remember how I used to be scared by how much your art consumed you? I would see how alone it could make you feel sometimes. Now I know you have too much of it to share for you to rest easy. Your art has allowed you to move on. I used to send you voice messages of me reading poetry because I wanted you to understand that I don't only hold my own stories but also all the words of the poets that explain my inner workings. Now my voice is in one of your tracks and I finally get to see you perform soon . The world that we made together is slowly leaking out.

In this autumn as the trees change colour and my hair grows long enough to touch the back of my neck for the first time, and my name changes, and sometimes when I shower I smile at myself in the mirror and sometimes it feels like I'm not waiting for you at all because I'm too busy looking at myself glimmering but then I remember that not all of this experience is mine, some of it is yours. As our gender has changed now, I think how beautiful it is that our love helped us become who we are.

I walk through the city and look at people and look at how they move together at intersections and how they glide past each other like passing touches and I wonder who it is that I haven't met yet.

Sometimes I get teary when the wind moves around me and through me and leaves are slowly falling and I think about how much of my past I'm letting go and this is the most present I've ever felt.

I know we all think about how we can change the world. I thought I needed to do that in my work. I know how you want to share your art with as many people as possible. But I want you to know how deeply you have changed my life. And I think that's all we are here to do. It is to show up, be in the moment, and love the people around us so deeply that our world does change.

Now I can walk into any room and feel held.

With love, always,
Kin

Kin Francis is a producer working with queer, Blak and POC communities. They are creating long-term projects and are developing their writing practice as a resident artist at Footscray Community Arts Centre. Kin's work has been funded by the Australia Council for the Arts, Creative Victoria, Asialink and Maribyrnong City Council.

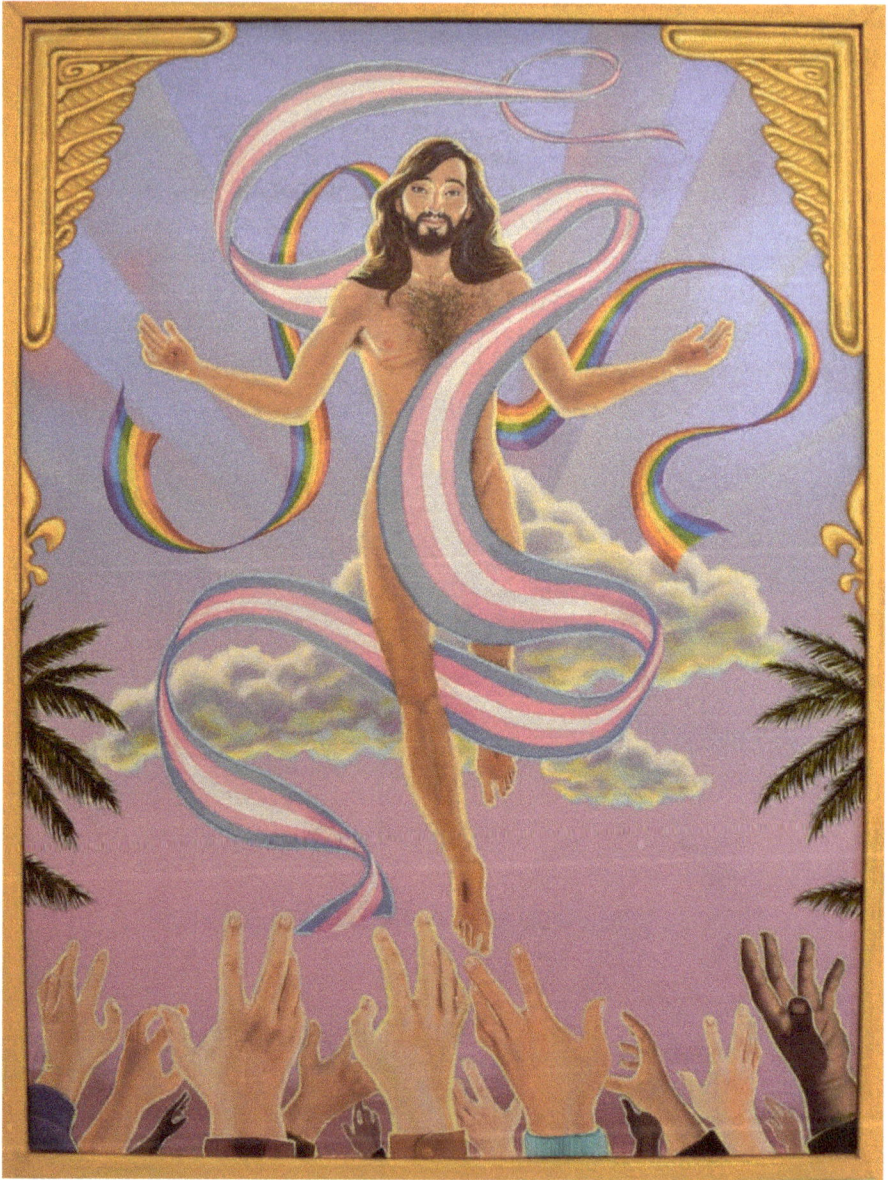

'The Ascension of Non-Cis Jesus' by Guy James Whitworth. This image features in a newly released collection of Guy's writing and painting, *Enough of Your Nonsense*, (Clouds of Magellan Press 2021). Guy is a co-founder of No Meat May and writes for *Sydney Sentinel*.

Build your archive armour for gender euphoria
REID MARGINALIA

Trans Exclusionary Radical Feminists and more transphobic people have been increasingly visible and vocal over the past few years. I have found myself retreating to the Australian archival material, most easily accessible online in 2020, in search of hope, support, solidarity, and liberation. It has made me think about:

- the role of queer and trans archivists and librarians in sustaining queer and trans community archives
- the role of queer and trans community archives in sustaining archivists and librarians who work in mainstream archives and libraries (and beyond), and
- the importance of knowledge sharing and collective archival action to help queer and trans communities stop history from repeating itself and construct a kind of archive armour.

Archie Barry describes 'archive armour' in 'Trans erasure, trans visibility: History, archives, and art' (Barry, 2018):

> It seems I've now naturally fallen into a role that many queer and gender-diverse people fall into: that of informal researcher. We silently horde content – URLs, zines, ads, pamphlets, stickers, mp3s, books, posters – to build a personalised buffer, a kind of archive armour, between the self and the cis-hetero world. Our ability to construct this type of armour is improving, as a number of new initiatives in archiving transgender histories emerge. The Digital Transgender Archive is the first accessible, global collection of documents relating to trans identities. The Canada-based international conference Moving Trans History Forward invites transgender and gender-non-conforming academics, writers, activists and archivists to discuss the cross-cultural preservation of gender-non-conforming histories.

Bringing back bibliographical babbling

I first came across the idea of bibliographical babbling via the Australian Queer Archives (AQuA) in one of the Gay libraryworkers group's newsletters from the 1970s. I loved it and thought it might be time to bring it back in online form:

> Many librarians are inveterate bower birds when it comes to printed matters gay, ending up with a veritable nest of quickly scribbled scraps, titles on used loan cards, and citations on beer coasters. But it would be all of much greater value if we could get it all together, and make it accessible to others. (Gay libraryworkers group, 1970+)

Inspired by this, I will now share a few sources that have helped me find hope, support, solidarity, and liberation in the archives and even more. They may help you construct your own kind of archive armour.

'Transsexual Liberation' by Ben Foreman and Susan Lewis in *Lesbianon* in 1975 via Reason in Revolt (Foreman & Lewis, 1975, p. 3):

> In response to our oppression, and the need to organise against it, a number of us, all transsexuals, have come together under the name of The Transsexual Action Organisation ... We extend our full support to the gay and women's movements because we are all fighting the same oppressor – a society which decrees that a person born male should behave one way and that a person born female in another. We also see ourselves in solidarity with the struggles of mental patients, blacks, prisoners and all other oppressed groups – for the liberation of one can only be achieved by the liberation of all.

There is also a piece in *Camp Ink* on transvestite and transsexual liberation in the US published in Australia in 1971 (Douglas, 1971). See '

There is a photograph of Roberta Perkins speaking at the Australian Transsexual Association (ATA) and Gay Solidarity protest in 1982 for more local evidence of trans liberation (AQuA, 1982). (Find out more about Roberta Perkins via the Roberta Perkins Law Project, LGBTIQ Legal Service, Ongoing).

Reading documents on trans liberation reminds me of this talk on 'The freedom to be: Marxism and trans liberation' by April Holcombe (Holcombe, 2021).

The *Boys Will Be Boys Newsletters* (Alex & Jasper, 1992-1993) collection available in the Digital Transgender Archive might be one of my favourite collections of all time. I found particular joy, support, and solidarity through reading the letters from subscribers who had found and connected with others like them. Alex and Jasper's *Boys Will Be Boys*, No.1 (February, 1992) … newsletter especially speaks to me (Alex & Jasper, 1992, p. 1):

> … Eight F2M boys have come to my attention within the last two months. Though seemingly a small number, compared to knowing only a handful previously and having met no-one before my gender change, this is quite incredible and only goes to show that there are more of us out there than we may well have imagined. Naturally, this is only the tip of a very isolated iceberg. Many of us are still feeling alienated or unsure of our decisions. Most of us lack sufficient information, especially medical, to better aid our decisions. All of us need support. For those of you on this mailing list please consider writing something of yourself and your experiences for others to read. Only first names will be used and naturally no addresses or phone numbers unless specifically given ·for publication will be printed. It's important that we share our thoughts, insecurities, excitement fears and knowledge. This group can only work if each individual is prepared to participate, even just a little. Don't leave this newsletter up to a dedicated few. This support group can have a far-reaching impact on the quality of our lives and the education of the community at large. You don't have to already have changed yourself physically yet, or ever intend to, to be involved. Your awareness of your male gender is all that is relevant …

Check out more issues of *Boys Will Be Boys* in the digital transgender archive (www.digitaltransgenderarchive.net).

I found a brief piece on Julie Peters running as a Federal election candidate in 1996 in Trove (LOTL Editorial, 1996, p. 7):

> Julie Elizabeth Peters [pictured] is believed to be the first endorsed lesbian transsexual candidate for a major political party

> … A director of photography at ABC TV, Peters, 44, concedes her chances of beating Labor candidate, ACTU president Martin Ferguson, are slim. But she says her candidature for the Australian Democrats is an important step for tranys.

Listen to Julie Peters on the Archive Fever (Claire & Yves, Various) and Transgender Warriors (Joy94.9, Various) podcasts and hear about her impressive personal archive and more.

Julie Peters' political endeavours reminded me of Georgina Beyer and I found her landslide New Zealand local council campaign victory reported in the *Canberra Times* (Editorial, 1995), which made me want to revisit this episode of the One From the Vaults podcast on her and the art of the possible (OFTV, 2015).

Searching Trove reminds me of the Transgender-related materials lists curated by librarian Anne (Rowland, 2018).

In turn, this reminds me of the talk 'Finding 'evidence of me' through 'evidence of us': Transgender oral histories and personal archives' speak' by Noah Riseman in which he shares oral histories and personal archives from even more transgender people from so called Australia (Riseman, 2020).

More to explore

- A history of LGBTIQ Victoria report (https://www.heritage.vic.gov.au/)
- Victoria's transgender history report (https://tgv.org.au/victorias-transgender-history-report)
- Australian Queer Archives (https://queerarchives.org.au/)
- Archiving the Aboriginal Rainbow (https://researchers.mq.edu.au/en/persons/andrew-farrell)
- Out of the Closet, Into the Streets (https://cv.vic.gov.au/stories/a-diverse-state/out-of-the-closets-into-the-streets/)
- Westandproud (https://www.facebook.com/westandproud
- Daylesford Stories (https://victoriancollections.net.au/stories/daylesford-stories)
- Hunter Rainbow History Group (https://livinghistories.newcastle.edu.au/nodes/view/59991)
- Small Town Queer (https://museum.tweed.nsw.gov.au/small-town-queer)

- Sydney Pride History Group (https://www.pridehistory.org.au/)
- Camp Ink 1970-1977 (https://nla.gov.au/nla.obj-757144341)
- Lesbians on the Loose 1990-1999 (https://catalogue.nla.gov.au/Record/263981)
- Gaywaves collection (https://timeline.nfsaa.com/gaywaves/)
- Garry Wotherspoon interviews, 1980-1988 (https://www.sl.nsw.gov.au/blogs/garry-wotherspoon-oral-history-interviews-gay-men-1980-1988-have-been-released-librarys-oral)
- Queering the Museum (https://queeringthemuseum.history.sa.gov.au/)
- Queering the collection (https://www.artgallery.nsw.gov.au/artsets/k35yvr)
- Trans Past, Trans Present: The Making Trans Histories Project (https://www.tepapa.govt.nz/)
- Pride NZ (http://www.pridenz.com/)
- Queering the map (https://www.queeringthemap.com/)
- Transgender Archives Discovery Tool (https://www.uvic.ca/transgenderarchives/discovery-tool/index.php)
- QZAP (https://www.qzap.org/v9/index.php)
- Adventures in time and gender (http://adventuresintimeandgender.org)
- Transgender warriors (https://joy.org.au/transgenderwarriors/)
- Queerstories (https://maevemarsden.com/queerstories/)
- Call me by my name (https://open.spotify.com/show/6cmaIVwiUyu2ngYIgrisTY)
- Counting the dead: Trans day of Remembrance podcast (https://gendercentre.org.au/counting-the-dead)
- Queer STEM History (https://queerstempodcast.wixsite.com/website)
- Digital archives and disruption (https://www.youtube.com/watch?v=4cgrPhHYMgg)
- We Weren't Born Yesterday (https://www.3cr.org.au/wewerentbornyesterday)
- Queer Indonesia Archive (https://www.qiarchive.org/)
- Cork LGBT Archive (https://corklgbtarchive.com/)

Becoming Reid Marginalia

I read and thought quite a lot about librarianship, particularly the teaching aspects, as a performance in 2019, and started 2020 by going to circus performance workshops which included drag, and participating in feral queer camp at Midsumma (https://feralqueercamp.com/). So, I went into lockdown thinking about lessons learned from performance to apply to teaching and taking them outside the academy (or going feral) and in October 2020 I presented as Reid Marginalia at work, and I have never felt more comfortable in myself and joyful than I did working like this. I still feel a sense of euphoria when listening to *The Logical Song* by Supertramp now – one of the songs I selected to get the presentation started inspired by the playlist provided by Dr Carolyn D'Cruz (2020) in her book *Democracy in Difference: Debating key terms of gender, sexuality, race and identity*.

An article on performance and librarianship that has resonated the most with me is 'Unpacking and overcoming 'edutainment' in library instruction' by Sarah Polkinghorne, as I am similarly quite critical of edutainment in the context of the marketisation of education (Polkinghorne, 2015). Some of the lessons from performance also resonated with the lessons I picked up from the performance workshop and feral queer camp. Polkinghorne illustrates that many of us feel like we are performing when we are teaching and reflects on aspects of performance that can help librarians create more engaging learning experiences while resisting edutainment. One of those aspects was physicality and this was the main focus of the performance skills workshop I did in order to help us become aware of and comfortable with our own bodies and voices and it has helped me move beyond 'solely cognitivist instructional strategies' and do less over-preparing in the library classroom like Polkinghorne (2015) suggests it can:

> Physicality is a broad term encompassing the ways in which we communicate with our bodies, through our postures and movements, expressions and gestures ... Our presence in the classroom is embodied. Even webinars are embodied, because we use our voices to deliver them. Comfort with our embodied presence is as fundamental to effective face-to-face teaching as it is to any performance.

Some of the parts of feral queer camp that resonated most perhaps not surprisingly involved the ACT UP teach in and ACT UP in conversation events at Hares and Hyenas where we learnt about and discussed the powerful ways ACT UP used street performance as a protest to raise awareness about the treatment of people with HIV/AIDS and discrimination against queer communities. Performance is emotive and can help make experiences, knowledges, theories, and information accessible to broader communities, outside academic institutions and help people understand experiences different from their own lived experiences. When discussing queer performances with fellow feral queer campers, *Gender Euphoria* (Davey et al., 2019) came up as an incredible joyful example and one of the most queer performances many of us had experienced.

The name Reid Marginalia came about as it sounds, quite GLAMorous! I love reading marginalia, as a way to connect with a text and its community of readers. I hope this piece can help others connect with texts and communities and find hope, support, solidarity, liberation, and euphoria.

Reid Marginalia is a librarian in a university by day and volunteer queer archivist by night. They are passionate about supporting independent community-based archives, encouraging critical, creative and collective reflection across the Gallery, Library, Archive and Museum (GLAM) sector and beyond it, and making critical knowledges, theories and histories accessible within and beyond the academy. If you enjoyed this piece, they encourage you to subscribe to bibliographical babbling for more: https://tinyletter.com/reidmarginalia/

References

Ahmed, S. (2010). *The Promise of Happiness*. Durham: Duke University Press.

Alex, & Jasper. (1992). Boys Will Be Boys Newsletter Editorial. *Boys Will Be Boys, 1*(1), 1. Retrieved from https://www.digitaltransgenderarchive.net/files/5712m662c

Alex, & Jasper. (1992-1993). Boys Will Be Boys Newsletters. *The Digital Transgender Archive, 1-2*(1,5,6,9,10,12,15 and 15). Retrieved from https://www.digitaltransgenderarchive.net/col/1r66j121q

AQuA (Ed.) (1982). *Photograph Roberta Perkins speaking at the Australian Transsexual Association (ATA) and Gay Solidarity protest Manly Sydney October 1982*. Melbourne: Australian Queer Archives.

Barry, A. (2018). Trans erasure, trans visibility: History, archives, and art. *Archer*. Retrieved from http://archermagazine.com.au/2018/11/trans-erasure/

Clare, & Yves. (Various). Live: Queering the Archive. *Archive Fever*. Melbourne: Archive Fever Pod.

D'Cruz, C. (2020). *Democracy in Difference: Debating key terms of gender, sexuality, race and identity*. Melbourne: La Trobe University EBureau.

Davey, M., Alto, M., Dixon, N., Leota Lu, A., Bailee-Rose , M., Fury, . . . Frankland, J. (2019). Gender Euphoria. Melbourne: Arts Centre Melbourne and Melbourne International Arts Festival.

Douglas, A. (1971). Transvestite and transsexual liberation in the US. *Camp Ink, 1*(8), 4-5.

Editorial. (1995). Landslide win for transsexual. *The Canberra Times*. Retrieved from https://trove.nla.gov.au/newspaper/article/130564338

Foreman, B., & Lewis, S. (1975). 'Transsexual Liberation', *Lesbianon, 1*(5), 3.

Gay libraryworkers group. (1970+). Bibliographical Babbling. *Gay libraryworkers newsletter*. Retrieved from https://queerarchives.org.au/

Holcombe, A. (2021). The freedom to be: Marxism and trans liberation. *Marx Talks*. Retrieved from https://marxtalks.com.au/talk/the-freedom-to-be-marxism-and-trans-liberation

Joy94.9. (Various). Transgender Warriors: Julie Peters. *Transgender Warriors*. Melbourne: Joy.org.au.

LGBTIQ Legal Service. (Ongoing). The Roberta Perkins Law Project. Retrieved from https://lgbtiqlegal.org.au/what-we-do/roberta-perkins-law-project/

LOTL Editorial. (1996). News Briefs: Trany Candidate. *Lesbians On The Loose, 7*(January), 7. Retrieved from https://nla.gov.au/nla.obj-1062344711/view?sectionId=nla.obj-1096042762&partId=nla.obj-1062436327#page/n6/mode/1up

OFTV. (2015). OFTV 6: The Art of The Possible. *One From the Vaults Podcast*. Sydney: Soundcloud.

Polkinghorne, S. (2015). Unpacking and overcoming 'edutainment' in library instruction. *In the Library With the Lead Pipe, 2015*. Retrieved from https://www.inthelibrarywiththeleadpipe.org/2015/edutainment/

Riseman, N. (2020). Finding 'evidence of me' through 'evidence of us': Transgender oral histories and personal archives' speak. *Transgender Histories*. Melbourne.

Rowland, A. (2018). Transgender related materials. *Trove*. Retrieved from https://trove.nla.gov.au/list/121446

I am free
STEVIE LANE

I didn't know gender for a long time.
We went to the same parties but had different friends,
Lived in the same town but at different ends.
To me, gender was deeply ingrained but always unseen.
A hot cup of coffee when all I drank was tea.
On the tip of my tongue, two steps ahead of me
But I could never…quite…catch up.

And while I couldn't quite put my finger on it,
Why being called a boy felt closer to home,
Than anyone I ever saw in the mirror.
Like a hot water bottle in bed on a cold winter's day
Or the smell of a home cooked meal, or some other cliché,
I played the game.
It wasn't fair, no one else cared, and no one answered my harrowing prayers,
But I played that game as if my life depended on it.
Because it did.

This narrative should not be common, but it is.
The one that says we are wrong, we don't belong
And we shouldn't exist
Kids killing themselves every day, or trying
Facing abuse on the frontline, breaking down and crying
We are led to believe we don't deserve unconditional love
That we must let the fear of being ourselves run through our veins
And wrap around our battered hearts until we slowly…fade…away.
That we should keep quiet or risk losing it all.
I was caught up in expectations of how I should look, act and feel
But not anymore.

I am not 'trapped in the wrong body'.
I don't owe you androgyny.
Gender is a construct, expressed unapologetically.
My heart feels warm under scars I wear proudly

My voice, deeper and stronger than all those trying to fix me

And don't talk about my resilience as if it's a valuable quality
It doesn't determine my strength, it was out of necessity.
Focus on dismantling the systems that oppress me
And my beautiful trans siblings that I forever strive to be.
Because trans joy really is an act of resistance,
Against this binary world that refuses to listen.
I will strive to share accounts of community and wisdom
For trans children need stories beyond narratives of victims
From the tales of our history to the paths that point north
Our voices echo loudly, calling the world forth

And at the end of the day, when it's all said and done,
I realise that in fact, I've known gender all along.
It has always been me, whatever I want it to be.
I may not have had the words, trans or non-binary
But I have always held the power to unlock my own truths.
I hold that key.
And finally, unequivocally,
I know I am free.

Stevie is a writer, videographer and digital creator based in Boorloo (Perth, WA). They have 10 years experience advocating for the rights of LGBTIQA+ people and other marginalised groups throughout Australia. They love to use their lived experience as a queer, trans and non-binary person to connect with others, educate and create change.

image: Jamie James

Joel

he him

Too busy for a quote but I'm thriving …

Seahorse
SUSAN LARDNER and JESSICA WARD

A History of The Seahorse Club

There have always been transgender people. For example, transgender depictions in art can be found from Mediterranean countries dating between 9000 to 3700 years ago, Sumerian texts from 2500 B.C document transgender priests known as gala, whilst Indian, Thai and North American cultures, just to name a few, have traditionally recognized transgender roles.

Modern western society particularly became more trans-aware in the latter half of the 20th century. There had been famous transgender individuals in the past, such as Elagabalus, the Chevalier d'Eon, the Abbe de Choisy, We'wha, James Barry and Lili Elbe, but certainly the most well-known trans person of the 1950s and 1960s was Christine Jorgenson. Her memoir, published in 1967, became a bestseller. Some would have heard of the transgender people previously mentioned, but Jorgenson really put the idea of gender fluidity much more firmly in the public consciousness. So, people who had inklings of their own gender fluidity now had heard of someone who was like them.

From tentative, but promising beginnings in the early 1970s, through subsequent years of membership complacency, sometimes inadequately staffed management committees, near extinction, near financial ruin, homelessness and infighting, to name but a few of the problems and difficulties that have beset the club over the years, Seahorse Victoria has survived, and can legitimately lay claim to being the longest continuously active transgender club in Australia and likewise, to being among a select few of the longest continuously active transgender clubs in the world.

It was in 1967 that Pauline Worner, a cross-dresser residing in Sydney and recently widowed, undertook through a lack of companionship to try and make contact with other cross-dressers. Her problem though was how to go about it. Prevailing societal attitudes meant that the very subject of transvestism was right there in the closet with the cross-dressers themselves. In fact, the situation was such that, being discovered dressed in public resulted in police action! Because of the conservative nature of society at this time, Pauline was unable to advertise, even discreetly, in the print media. As it happened, she was acquainted with a man named Jack Fischer who operated a discreet mail order business, advertising in the *Australasian Post* magazine to supply 'special' items. She wrote to Jack and asked if he could put her in touch with other cross-dressers.

Through her inquiry to Jack Fischer, Pauline soon came to be in contact with Joan Kempthorne of New Zealand, who in turn knew Rosemary Langton of Melbourne, and Carole, a ship's officer from the UK who visited Sydney fairly regularly. This small group corresponded and, early in 1968, Joan, Rosemary and Pauline met up for the first time in Sydney. Over dinner they discussed the possible numbers of other cross-dressers who could be in town and who could be joining them for dinner. They decided to do something about making contact and possibly establishing some type of club.

Their first newspaper advertisement was as explicit as possible for the times: 'TV enthusiast would like to meet people with similar views and interests.' About 30 replies were received, among them being enthusiasts of, you guessed it, television! There were some cross-dressers though who came forward and this encouraged the group to advertise again in 1969. From these tentative beginnings enough cross-dressers came together to form the nucleus of a club.

Inspired by the United Kingdom's Beaumont Society, and following many informal meetings and much discussion, a framework was established and ultimately the official, inaugural meeting of the club took place in Sydney in 1970. The name Seahorse was adopted, and The Seahorse Club of Australia was born in 1970. The Club adopted a constitution and elected its first committee in 1971, from the outset promoting itself as a national club for cross-dressers.

Through her work, in the RAAF, making her quite good at 'getting off the ground', Pauline Worner frequently travelled around Australia and in time she was able to follow up inquiries from interstate cross-dressers who had responded to the Sydney advertising. Meeting individuals and conducting interviews, Pauline recruited 'country' members of the Sydney-based club and thus the first steps were taken towards setting up branches of the club in firstly Melbourne, followed by Adelaide, Brisbane and Perth. So, thanks in large part to Pauline following up interstate inquiries, the membership became national, with representatives dubbed 'counsellors' based in the other states, acting as the leaders of the non-Sydney groups.

In Melbourne, an attempt at establishing a cross-dressing club got under way in 1971. In August of that year, a Melbourne branch of the national Seahorse began gathering at the home of Karen; her flat in Kew became known as 'Kew Castle'. The group does not appear to have gotten off to a very auspicious start. According to Lady Paula Howard, an English-born cross-dresser who gave herself a title, the group appears to have numbered no more than about four. Early on, it was difficult to build numbers. Writing in a Seahorse newsletter in the late 1970s, Lady Paula said that when she came to the scene in Melbourne, there was barely even the pretence of a club, that's how small the numbers were. For example, she refers to the fact that an attempt to have a party to celebrate the first anniversary of the club in 1972 failed through a lack of interest and non-attendance.

One of the big difficulties for the growth of such a club was that public cross-dressing was still a very, very dangerous activity in the 70s. If someone drove to or from a meeting dressed, they no doubt feared being spotted, attacked, or even being subject to police harassment. Cross-dressing was illegal. To not have at least three items of male clothing on was a criminal offence for an MTF Trans person, in those days. Most members in these early days would pack their clothes in their cars and would dress at the venue to minimise risk.

From early in 1973 though, it appeared, for a time, that things might be on the improve. In an article in the first edition of *Feminique* (c. February 1973) Karen is referred to as bringing 'some cheerful news from Melbourne; it appears that the southern club has moved out of its former doldrums. The membership is on the increase following a recent advertisement.' By this time, Karen was recognized as the Melbourne representative of the Sydney-based national club. In the second edition of *Feminique* (c.April 1973) she is listed as such with the club executive.

Despite these indications in early 1973 of better prospects for the group, it appears any progress was short-lived. The failure of the group up until the start of 1973 dampened Karen's enthusiasm for any formal structure for the group. Thereafter, while Karen continued to play hostess at 'Kew Castle', it was on the basis that the group met for 'informal gatherings'. The members of the group apparently concurred, there was no interest in committing to the establishment of a branch of the national club, or of setting up a separate Melbourne club either. Local and interstate visitors continued to be entertained as and when they infrequently attended and generally the group, or rather Karen, tried to widen the circle of cross-dressing contacts in Melbourne.

Independently of what was happening in Sydney and at 'Kew Castle', with Seahorse affiliates, other transgendered individuals were placing advertisements in the Victorian newspapers looking for like-minded individuals, and they managed to connect with each other and hold social gatherings. A particular social 'leader' in this area was Robyn Payne.

Robyn had been busy herself contacting and meeting other local Melbourne crossdressers. For example, it seems that at some stage around 1971, Robyn had replied to a 'sad and troubled letter' from a cross-dresser that appeared in the Truth newspaper column of Fr. Glover. In return, Robyn was inundated with responses from about 30 people seeking friendship and advice, or to share cross-dressing experiences. Corresponding with these people over a period resulted in Robyn forming a 'small, exclusive club', an informal social and support contact group.

Subsequently, Robyn came across an advertisement in a fringe magazine pertaining to the Sydney based Seahorse Club. The advertisement described the club as a national TV organisation. She wrote and applied for membership, but got no response. Some months later Robyn advertised herself in the fringe magazine and was duly contacted by Karen of 'Kew Castle'. Liaising with Sydney as she was, Karen was able to refer Robyn for membership of the club.

Over the ensuing months through 1973, Robyn attended the informal meetings at 'Kew Castle' on a number of occasions. Her group and the Victorians who had joined NSW Seahorse soon came together. In January 1974, Robyn replaced Karen as the Melbourne representative of the Sydney based club, being appointed as the Melbourne 'counsellor'. Following her appointment, Robyn set about the task of establishing a viable Melbourne branch of the club. Taking her appointment seriously and building on the work she had already commenced independently, she gathered together a small group of likewise enthusiastic followers. The group initially began meeting at Robyn's home with subsequent meetings farmed out to the homes of other members of the group. If not yet on a monthly basis, the meetings were held somewhat more regularly than had been the case at Kew. Also, unlike Kew, where the meetings were informal and social, Robyn's meetings were intended to have both a social and support basis, developing at least the beginnings of a sense of formality and seriousness and a sense of purpose in reaching out to and providing for the needs of cross-dressers.

By early to mid-1975, Robyn's group had developed to the extent that a distinct feeling began to emerge that the group was big enough and organised enough to be able to stand alone as a club in its own right, separate from but still affiliated with the Sydney based national club.

This 'independence movement' was prompted, it seems, by a sense of isolation from the national club. It was felt that the Victorian branch of NSW Seahorse needed their own organisational structure and leadership, to direct their local activities. There was apparently a distinct lack of communication from the Sydney based executive, (in one historical article in *Seahorse Times*, reference is made to the club being notorious for not responding to membership inquiries in particular) and there was a view that, although the club tried to promote its national status, it was too Sydney-centric. This was particularly evident in the club magazine, *Feminique*, which devoted much of its content to social events and happenings in Sydney, with branch news from other States being minimal. (It could be argued though, that the magazine was only as good and as balanced as its contributors). A sense of frustration and dissatisfaction arose within the Melbourne group, a repeated comment, particularly in relation to paying membership fees to Sydney, was: 'We got nothing for our money.' For some reason, Seahorse Victoria traditionally celebrates its birthday in June each year, despite the fact that this inaugural meeting of the Club was actually held in September 1975.

One member of Robyn's group who joined her from Kew Castle was Vivienne Clarke. She apparently played a leading role with Robyn in developing the cohesive spirit of the group such that, she is credited with being the one who was instrumental in marshalling the group to hold the first Seahorse Victoria meeting in September 1975. A small group of five or six people gathered at the home of Sharon Holden, a flat in St. Kilda; the initial membership list drafted in October 1975 had twelve names. An interim steering committee comprised Robyn Payne as secretary and Vivienne Clarke as treasurer and they were joined in December by Jo-Anne Cooper as president. At the outset, meetings were scheduled to be held on a regular monthly basis and, to keep the members informed, Robyn began production (from August 1975) of a monthly newsletter. This was a one- or two-page publication designed to keep members informed of meeting dates and venues as well as other news and information.

Membership of the newly formed Seahorse Victoria was conditional on also being a paid-up member of the national club and, for a time, Seahorse Victoria promoted itself as being affiliated with the national club, with the aims and constitutions of the two clubs being the same.

With increasing membership and attendances at meetings, the Club quickly outgrew the confines of Sharon's St. Kilda flat. As from November or December the Club began meeting at the President Motor Inn on Queens Rd, Melbourne, initially occupying the bridal suite. Long standing member Lyn Taverner recalls being the one responsible for the nerve-wracking, heart-stopping experience of checking in to the motel's reception desk on behalf of the Club to collect the key to the room.

In February 1976, the committee held its first official meeting and, at a subsequent general meeting the members voted formally to ratify the September 1975 separation from the national body. The Seahorse Club of Victoria was thus officially launched.

Copies of *Seahorse Victoria – 45 Years A Retrospective* are available for purchase from Seahorse Victoria.

http://seahorsevic.com.au

T-wenty20: Lockdown Island
TIARN

2020 has been intense. In so many ways it has been tragic, scary, saddening, confusing, and has disrupted life as we knew it.

2020, the year of: devastating Australian bushfires. The impeachment and acquittal of President Trump. Joe Biden winning the US Election. Kamala Harris becoming the first African American woman and the first Asian American woman on a major party's presidential ticket, leading to her becoming the first female, black, and Asian American vice president. The Black Lives Matter protests. The Beirut explosion. Scientists discovering a parasitic microbe that blocks mosquitos from carrying malaria. Ruth Bader Ginsburg's death. The California wildfires. The United Kingdom withdrawing from the European Union. Mining corporation Rio Tinto admitting to blowing up the 46,000-year-old Juukan Gorge caves in Western Australia. Costa Rica becoming the first Central American country to legalise same-sex marriage. NASA confirming the existence of molecular water on the sunlit side of the Moon. The former Mayor of Nyakizu Ladislas Ntaganzwa being sentenced to life imprisonment for his role in the Rwandan genocide. The sacred Djab Wurrung Directions Tree being destroyed by the Victorian government for a Western Highway upgrade. The global coronavirus pandemic. And the year I started testosterone.

That last event may seem tiny in relation to the rest of the events; insignificant in comparison to the worldwide effect of the other events. But here is why it is cataclysmic in relation to my existence. I live on the un-ceded land of the Wurundjeri people, in Victoria, Australia. We have just started to get back to some normality after more than four months of lockdown; months of not seeing family and friends, of having no work hours, and questioning what each day will look like. I truly believe that such drastic action was required in response to the covid-19 pandemic outbreak in Victoria; and we are already seeing the fruits of this action, 42 consecutive 'double doughnut' days (0 new cases, and 0 deaths – as of 11th December 2020). As someone who suffers anxiety and depression the total upturning of my weekly routine and the introduction of new social protocols significantly affected me. I went into the pandemic lockdown with grand plans, lists of projects, and self-improvement activities to fill my time; I am coming out of the pandemic lockdown with several unfinished projects, too much knowledge about beekeeping for someone who shouldn't be stung by bees, a higher dosage of anti-depressants, and the new knowledge of book binding. However, the one accomplishment that I will always remember and associate with 2020, is the joy of starting Testosterone.

You see, I am non-binary, trans masculine to be more specific; and I NEVER thought I would start T. I didn't want to. And I swore I would never start it based off social dysphoria and misgendering. Up until lockdown I was against my starting T because 'it wouldn't be for me' and 'I wasn't going to do it for the benefit of others'. But lockdown changed my whole perspective and understanding of my thoughts and emotions, in relation to this topic.

During my Gender Clinic sessions, my psych had asked questions along these lines: 'if you were on a desert island, with no one else around, no one to view your body, label you, misgender you, pressure you, what would you want your body to look like? How do you feel your body should already be? How would you feel most comfortable in your physicality?'

It is a helpful thought exercise to help you discern 'what you want' vs 'external pressure and/or expectations'. I already knew I would not/should not have breasts, but the rest was either undecided, or a blur – a literal pixelated image in my head – I just couldn't envision it. I thought this was because I didn't care, or have a desire; I was wrong. Even during this thought exercise, fear of society ate its way into my being.

Lockdown became my 'desert island' – no misgendering from strangers, no feeling overexposed in bathers in a highly binary gendered workplace, no misgendering from managers, co-workers, kids I teach or their parents; no judgement from conservative Christian family members – and the thought of bodily changes that would occur from testosterone crept into my mind. They caught me off guard in a peaceful, contentment-filled way. So, I went with it. I allowed myself to entertain the idea of bottom growth, facial hair, voice drop; and the more I allowed myself to consider these things, the more I craved them. I had thought that my previous moments of desire to start testosterone were only because society was getting to me, causing me pain because I didn't fit 'the binary norm' (driven by frustration and dysphoria). Instead it turns out that I was scared to face society, exist in society, be viewed as a laboratory experiment by society while starting T. This realisation was joyful, exciting, and unexpected, and with it came a sense of urgency to start testosterone! If I was ever going to start T, it would be now, during a worldwide pandemic, in lockdown, 'on my desert island'. It was for me, no one else, and only my direct family and most trusted friends would be informed. The others would find out either when our paths crossed again, or when I was comfortable to share my story with the world. This was my journey, and on my 'desert island' no one could spoil my joy of starting testosterone. My housemates threw me a 'T-party' the day of my first shot, and no one could try and convince me that this was a bad choice, or sinful, or wrong. I was ecstatic and had nothing but total support coming my way from my partner, direct family, and closest friends.

It is an odd feeling to be grateful for a state-wide pandemic lockdown. I have even felt shame for being grateful for this 'desert island' I ended up on. But I have had to remind myself regularly, with the help of my partner and friends, that there is a big difference between being grateful for the space I was given to become more myself and being grateful for the pandemic as a whole. The latter would be cataclysmically fucked up; the former speaks a truth about my experience as a non-binary human existing and living on this planet. 2020 has been a 'shit-show' and across the globe too many lives have been lost, and too many terrible events have occurred. But 2020 is also the year that I was given a 'desert island' and I started testosterone; and I will always be grateful, and feel joy when thinking of that. Both of these statements are true, and both of them can exist at once. The world is a messy place, and terrible stuff happens, but moments of joy and freedom can occur within it all. Sometimes we all need a 'desert island' – a reprieve from it all – I hope you can find yours; because I was lucky to find mine, and I will be forever grateful for it.

Now with restrictions easing, and the ability to see more people becoming a reality, I am once again dreading being misgendered by strangers, facing the judgement of conservative family members, navigating public toilets and change rooms, and trying to find a new job. It's overwhelming more often than not, it feels harder than prior to lockdown, it is more draining than prior to lockdown; I have become more 'sensitised' to these experiences. I have lost my 'thick skin' that I wore daily prior to lockdown – and although I don't want said 'thick skin' back, I am also not sure how I will navigate society now without it. Is it possible to maintain my new-found sense of freedom, peace, and joy about my daily changing body, while navigating a society that rarely accounts for my non-binary existence (let alone my now changing body)? This is a question and a reality I will have to face daily. But I have the solace of navigating it all with finally having learnt more about myself, my desires, and the physicality in which I need to move through the world. Now I just have to let the T do its work. And take each day at a time.

Tiarn is a non-binary, queer human living on Wurundjeri land, in Victoria. They are a passionate advocate for the safety and affirmation of LGBTIQA+ Christians, volunteering with the Brave Network. They are a storyteller, cat-parent, and creative person who loves D&D, video games, woodwork, and coffee.

Best Day Worst Day Podcast

Interview with CB Mako

Best Day, Worst Day is a podcast where I take the time to have a chat with a
different LGBTIQA+ activists and creatives and ask them to tell me about a good day
and a bad day they've had. Their stories have been fascinating. This is an excerpt of
my interview with CB Mako. In this interview, cubbie discussed their experience of
disability as a non-binary person of colour, fanfiction, marriage equality and
patriarchal structures.

— Sam Elkin

CB Mako: My name is CB Mako. My friends called me cubbie. My
pronouns are cubbie or they/them. I am a migrant and person of
colour. I'd like to acknowledge that I live on stolen unceded lands of
the Wurundjeri and Boon Wurrung people of the Kulin nation. I pay
my respects to their elders past, present and emerging. Always was,
and always will be Aboriginal Land.

Thanks Sam, for inviting me onto this amazing podcast. And
thank you for transcribing your podcasts, it's so important and rare.

Sam Elkin: Thanks for joining me on Best Day, Worst Day.

CB Mako: Yes, so, worst day and best day, okay, let's see… well are
living in year two of the apocalypse. The global pandemic is still
happening. Even though here in Naarm, we are currently at zero
cases, it's a very different situation outside of Australia.

Probably the best day ever as a writer was at the program launch
of Writers Victoria on 7th December 2017. I was a member of
Writers Victoria, and there was an invitation to attend the launch of
their new summer program. Back then, I've always been active in
attending literary events. That was one of the things I'd love to do.
And the program launch was a free event with free food. I don't say
no to free food!

We were up on the second floor of The Wheeler Centre where all
the drinks and food were laid out. And just as they were launching
their new program for 2018, the Same Sex Marriage Bill was passed
on the final sitting day of the year in federal Parliament. Everyone just

broke down; we were all in tears. That was the best feeling ever because I felt that I was in a safe space and I could think about what it meant for the future generation, my kids. I couldn't wait to tell my kids when I got home.

Sam Elkin: What made you think about what it meant for future generations?

CB Mako: I told my kids (who were assigned female at birth) that they can be whatever they want to be when they grow up. When one of my kids went to high school, they wore boys' uniforms throughout. Since then, I've raised them as non-binary. I've also met with other queer parents who are raising non-binary teens. We follow each other on social media and even met face-to-face after the pandemic lockdown to catch up on how things are with our teenagers. We were all trying our best to give them the privileges that we didn't have when we were growing up. We had to hide behind the patriarchy just to keep us safe.

Sam Elkin: Can you tell us more about that?

CB Mako: I grew up in a time of martial law in the Philippines, where it was very traditional. I could not express anything about myself outside of the binary system. I had cousins who were non-binary, and they were kicked out of their parents' houses. I don't know what happened to them. So, that showed me, 'okay, I better keep quiet'.

Going back to the evening of 7th December 2017, someone told me there was going to be an anthology for Growing up Disabled in Australia. Though it took a while for me to submit an entry, it was fantastic when my poem got accepted!

So, there were two great things in one day on 7th December 2017.

Everyone was just in a party mood after that. There were drinks flowing. It was just a joy! We were all crying at the same time because it was a joyous event. Because waiting had been torturous, having to go through the referendum.

Sam Elkin: The postal survey?

CB Mako: Yes, that. That was too much. especially since (the politicians) could just vote on it straight away without it. Now I look forward to a better life for the next generation, for my kids. Unfortunately, I'm trapped in this patriarchy. I have to keep quiet inside my household. Because I'm inside a patriarchal structure, I cannot get out of it as much as I want to. The structures in government are very patriarchal as well. So, I just have to keep quiet.

I wear different hats. When I am on my own, or out as a writer in the writer's environment, I can be myself. But when I am inside the household it feels like it's a performance. I struggle to maintain strictly delineated roles. These strict roles have been passed on through the generations, and that's the expectation in my colonized culture, unfortunately. The culture where I grew up in.

Sam Elkin: What is it like for you in the world of writing?

CB Mako: When you're a writer, you read a lot. You learn a lot. It opens your mind. And now, I'm far away from the country where I was born, I can some make decisions away from the patriarchs of the clan.

As a writer, I consider myself non-binary. I'm one of the four founding members of the Disabled QBIPOC Collective. There's myself, Pauline Vetuna, Hannah Morphy-Walsh, and Gemma Mahadeo. All of us are queer and we all have disabilities as well, which is a kind of trifecta of intersections. You've got gender, race, and disability in one Collective.

So, discussing the three intersections is one goal. It's a bit tricky, but we try to answer that gap in the discussions. For example, you're in a BIPOC event or a queer event, but there's no accessibility – and this happens a lot. The event organisers make excuses and say they don't have a budget, or, 'Oh, sorry, we didn't think of it. And it's too late now because we already rented this venue'. Or they say, 'Sorry, we donated all our budget somewhere else. There's no budget to add accessibility, whether Auslan, captions, or transcription'.

We're still asking for basic inclusion. We're trying to insert ourselves into the narrative and say, 'Hey, we exist as queer BIPOC disabled artists and writers!'

People of colour usually don't want to express that they have a disability. Many have approached me privately on social media and disclosed that they have a disability but that they aren't open to discussing it on social media because of the backlash they will receive from their families or their friends. Particularly around mental health issues, which can be an invisible kind of disability. Have you heard of the term 'model migrant?'

Sam Elkin: Vaguely?

CB Mako: Everybody wants to be the model migrant. I'm not your model migrant. To legitimise my disability, I even secured a loan just to have a formal assessment for Autism. They – clinical psychologists – diagnosed me with Asperger's, or what they call nowadays 'Level 1 Autism Spectrum Disorder' or ASD. This wasn't picked up when I was growing up. I got my formal diagnosis just before the pandemic. When I told that to my parents, they just laughed. They just couldn't believe I'm autistic. So, it can be difficult for a person of colour to prove that they have an invisible disability in their community. You have to go through all these extra things to prove that you are legitimately disabled.

Sam Elkin: Tell us how you got into writing.

CB Mako: It all started with fanfiction. It was winter of 2012, and I was stuck alone at home with a toddler who was recuperating from chemotherapy. I didn't know what to do. Then I found out that this giant robot called Voltron was on the local television channel ABC Me, and I was like, 'Oh, gosh! they're back!'

I grew up with Voltron. That was the only cartoon my mum would let me watch. And only because there was a pink princess in the cartoon. I wasn't allowed to watch Transformers or play with Transformers toys because I was assigned female at birth. And I was so annoyed with that. So, I stuck with Voltron because there's a pink princess. But I was very fascinated with giant robots.

So, I started writing Voltron fanfiction. But most of the other Voltron fanfiction writers were from the USA. So, I was looking around for local writers and I discovered that there's a whole other side of Melbourne, the 'City of Literature'. And next thing you know, I was attending events at Writers Victoria.

I submitted an entry to a writing competition where I wrote about my experience of having a toddler with cancer. And next thing I knew, I was among ten winners who were offered a spot to attend a six-month writing workshop with author Lee Kofman at Library at the Dock in Docklands. Since then, I've been published in literary journals, performed at literary festivals and recently contributed to two anthologies: *Growing up Disabled in Australia*, which was edited by Carly Findlay. The other one is *Collisions: Fictions of the Future*, which is a futurist speculative fiction collection featuring First Nations writers and writers of colour.

Listen to the rest of CB Mako's interview or read the full transcript at https://bestdayworstday.com.au/. CB Mako is a non-fiction, fiction, and fanfiction writer and a member of the Disabled QBIPOC Collective. Their work is published in *Collisions* (Pantera Press), and *Growing Up Disabled in Australia* (Black Inc. Books).

You
NAT HOLLIS

You'll pick up skating, to try and cure it – the feeling that sometimes your hands aren't even your own – not even the kind of skating that would allow you to emulate the figures of masculinity you deified as a teenager, this will be *roller* skating, because you saw Elliot Page doing it in a movie once, and you're just monkey-see monkey-do with anything he does (including but not limited to: kissing women, pretending to be one of the X-Men, and weirdly wanting to fuck Michael Cera).

The smart thing to do is to start skating in the summer, so you can learn while sliding down oceanside paths wearing crop tops and enjoying the idle sun wasting itself away on shoulders that haven't seen the open air for six months. This is not what you will do.

You will start skating in the winter. Which means a good skate is a day where halfway through your little sliding trek past the cemetery, which stretches miles longer than any cemetery you've ever seen before, you will strip the puffy winter coat that you layered on to cope with the chill. And once you've peeled it from your now sweet, sweat-sticky skin, you'll tie it around your waist and marvel at how suddenly feminine your silhouette becomes. And maybe you'll be happy like that for a half second. *Maybe*. And that's on a good day.

What does a bad day look like then? That's the obvious question, because god sorry but sweat sticky skin being the highlight of a day that probably doesn't come around enough doesn't sound all that appealing. I know.

A bad day, then, is when it's raining. The days when, even though you love to skate and you love the rain, the combination of these two things brings you such a vapid sadness that you'll wonder what the point of anything at all is.

About halfway down the concrete path beside the cemetery you'll find yourself stuffed into skates a half-size small that you're rather happy about because have you tried getting skates nowadays? Especially ones for feet as big as yours. Not that they haven't been on you the whole time, just now you notice it, now you come somewhere close to feeling them.

Sometimes you won't remember putting them on.

It's like how you'd imagine pregnancy almost. Don't your feet swell in pregnancy? And don't you feel alien in your flesh? That's how you think about it anyway, when you're lying in bed at night sometimes, wishing the thing was *physical* physical. That it could be conveyed to anyone else in the world. Or maybe it's nothing at all like pregnancy, you just have Page on the brain and you're thinking about Juno.

But that doesn't matter.

Anyway it's raining, not pissing, but just kind of gentle. You think it's gentle anyway, any definite feeling would require the removal of the helmet that exaggerates the size of your head to a preposterous level, and there are days where that is an option, but this is not one of them. Because rainy days are the days where you are prone to falling. Not just falling either, but falling bad. Falling where you feel the world spin and ache as you rocket downwards towards it. Falling where, at it's worse, you get caught in the motion of it. Where the Whole Fear is with you and you are with it in the moment for what feels like indefinitely. So then, of course, you'll be skating laden in more protective gear than just the helmet, but whatever combination of knee, shin, or elbow pads that felt right for the day, plus the possibility of a mouthguard, and some glasses (though maybe not, because if you don't keep your head down they're liable to get all spattered with rain), and maybe even gloves if you feel particularly scared. You'll feel misshapen and exaggerated all wrong by everything you've laden on. Because something about falling in the cold, in the winter months, makes it ache even more, makes it even more disheartening to fall down.

This day … sorry not this day, the day I'm really thinking about when I describe this to you, *that* day, you were decked out in it all, because you were scared, *really* scared, for no particular reason, just that falling didn't appeal at all. And you were fairly confident you would pass only a few people , so the outward impacts of looking half like a fool, with your body made out of proportion, didn't matter so much as the internal security of the very real protection. So just imagine something like *that* day, filled with rain and fear, because that's what I'm doing anyway and it's probably good if we're on the same page.

On the bad days, or at least this bad day, you're so connected to the ground, so enamoured by the looking down, so absorbed by the Nothing Much At All, you won't see the little pile of now muffled feathers plastered to the ground. Will hardly feel the gentle mush and thud of wheels passing over and gathering detritus. There's not enough feeling left in you, you don't think. Not even enough for physical things. Can't notice the sharp incline of a too close corpse, let alone feel sad for it, feel the weight of the thing that once chirped and whirred with life now wrapped around your wheels … not on a bad day.

Anyway, all that doesn't matter.

So you're skating on slippery ground, covered by every protection you could gather, even though a very large part of the whole skating thing is how nice it makes you feel about how you look, like almost angelic gliding along free of restraint. But you forgo that for the protection. There is no euphoria, only … whatever the opposite of euphoria is.

And then you go past the cemetery, further than you normally would, in hopes of finding the joy you normally get. Or not even joy, rather contentedness, euphoria in the sense that you don't even notice that you're flying once you get going, of simultaneously being entirely yourself, and not at all in your own body. But what you won't realise, or remember from the last time, is that the path past the graveyard isn't as nice, it takes you into one of those neighbourhoods where the footpaths aren't so well taken care of, where the cracks in the sheets of concrete are filled by that gravel-y amalgam material. Which is perfectly fine if you're walking but is really truly hell to skate on. Especially in too tight skates. Because then your toes are pushed even more into themselves. And you just *know* the one toenail that's turned black already, but doesn't hurt so bad, will be peeling itself away from your foot with joy as it yawns back down into the soft string of flesh tearing away underneath. And then maybe you get it. Or think you get it. You'll think that maybe you're, deep down, not all that capable of having a deep down, and you're just an empty body or maybe shallow souled. And what then? What do you do with that information now that you're on shaky, slippery ground, protected from head to toe but not even feeling it, actually feeling more vulnerable than ever. All because in a rashness you've put yourself in a position of even greater danger just to try and rid yourself of this … this… anti-euphoria (anti because it's not just the absence of euphoria. Because the *presence* of euphoria is in the not noticing it, the *lack* of it must also be the present antithesis of it (… to an extent (… I've confused myself)). And what do you even do?

That's a bad day. You end up in the shower trying to pull chill and wet from your bones, holding on to the railing, all blood rush and yearning to bend over backwards once the heat and the steam get too much but just can't quite seem to make yourself turn the temperature down because then where are you? At least you feel half-alive with your hair curling, face blistering, heat. Feel half alive because you can believe you are at least an empty body, feel at least the presence of those hands you're not sure are even yours anymore. And if you feel half alive you feel halfway closer to the good days and god any connection to the good days is something to be held with a fetishistic reverence. Because at least on the good days you'll have the half a second of positivity and presence of mind to really feel your surroundings. It is then that the possibility ... not just the possibility actually, the real tangible promise of days better than good, of summer days, and sun, and comfortability at some point in the future, feels uncompromisable, prophesied even. Like some great deity has written your extant happiness into the stars and no matter how hard the intangible tries, you will never not make it to that point. No matter how much the days pass with liquid demeanour and ill intent you will never not see summer days again.

Some days, the ones that go beyond bad, you'll sit. Take in the hot water in long, sad draughts, feel it on the breathes in and nothing at all on the breathes out. And you'll wash blood from the skates still on your feet. You'll use the same sour, stinging brush to clean you and your shoes. Rinsing it in short bursts. Scraping away blood and grime and feather until you're so focussed that clean spittle drips down from your mouth and mixes with the soapy wash and redness. You're too intent to worry about appearance, or blood, or the bruises that have steadily formed from falling. Though, I suspect, even if you were somewhere closer to your body, the latter wouldn't worry you. You are not about the business of old bruises. If anything, all this proves that. Because you must, somewhere, beyond all this, have the faith that the old bruises cannot hold forever. And that someday, even though there seems to be nothing more than Nothing More, the bright warmth of summer days will cradle you like it does so many others.

Nat Hollis is a non-binary/transfem emerging writer from so-called regional WA. They worked as an economics tutor before moving to Naarm to study sociology and creative writing, and to pursue a career as a novelist. Nat writes and edits for Farrago Magazine and is currently finishing their first novel.

Don't ask don't tell
ROWAN RICHARDSON

What's your name mate?

I hesitate. Look up at mum. My head barely reaching her waist, my hand reaching up to grasp hers.

Jo.

My name hangs in the air. Heavy. I can feel mum tense. But she stays silent. A complicit accomplice in my masculine pseudonym, she gives me a nod to join an older group of kids that are playing cricket.

Hey Jo! Wanna bat?

Jo follows me around. Every new acquaintance, especially fleeting ones, are given the full Jo treatment. A home-schooled boy who lives on a farm, wears a Bart Simpson hat, that loves dinosaurs, cricket, and matchbox cars. My parents play along in public, but never enter the game. At home I am never a boy. I am never Jo.

I start 'real' school in grade 5. Jo is put in a cupboard and never let out again. The school uniform - a blue tartan dress - blocks the exit to the cupboard door. At school, I am constantly peppered with the same old question.

Are-you-a-boy-or-a-girl?

My name becomes irrelevant. I am repulsed by the girls who play with skipping ropes. The boys are repulsed by me; a threat in a dress. I relearn my mannerisms, my speech, my walk, my laugh. I feel like I'm lying all the time. More than I ever was as Jo.

If you repeat a lie enough it eventually becomes truth. That's what I repeated to myself anyway.

Are you a lesbian or something?

High school. A catholic high school, no less. My lies are woven over me so tightly I can no longer determine the truthful weft or the lying warp of my fabric. The threads that I can reach are washed religiously and wrung out. Almost daily. I shave my legs. My hair is long and heavy. My tartan dress is replaced with a maroon skirt and tie, but the tie is small and shorter than the boys. I bury myself in sports a girl should play. Which shockingly, also require a skirt.

We don't care if you are gay we just want to know. Well?

I play the constant cat and mouse game of succeeding and then failing to not draw attention to myself. Everyone knows there's something wrong with me. My friends wait for me to slip up and expose what I truly am with baited breath. A dirty lesbian. Transgender wasn't even a word that people knew in country NSW in the early naughties. 'Shim', however, was used like a slingshot to any person who deigned step out of their boy/girl box.

You're not one of those gross butch lesbians are you?

I scoff in response. Gross. Butches. *If I wanted to date a man I would date a real one.* My hair is long. I've fallen in love and had my heart broken already. I'm at university. I'm worldly and so alone. I obsess over my weight, my skin, my clothes. They never look right. Like I've somehow picked up the wrong skin from the gym changing room floor and worn it home without noticing.

I love your breasts. Why would you want to chop them off?

I cautiously float the idea of breast reductions to partners. It sinks like a stone. I toy with the idea of being 'butch'. I take the plunge and cut my hair. Everyone loves it, including me. I start wearing men's underpants, the only menswear that my partner at the time approves of because they make my legs look 'skinny'.

Are you a lesbian?

My first day as a teacher. Term 1, week 1, day 1 of grade 9 science at a Tasmanian country public school. We are drawing comics to introduce ourselves but the only person who doesn't know anyone in the room is me. Somehow, the combination of my men's clothes and story about enjoying motorbikes has betrayed me for the raging queer that I am within the first 10 minutes. I pause after the question is asked. I know the aims of the question, asked by a 'bad boy' trying to challenge my authority, prove himself, and make me uncomfortable - three birds with four words. The atmosphere of the class is mixed but tense, like they don't know whether they are sitting in the past, present or future. It makes them very nervous.

I smile and say Of course, can't you tell?

In that scholastic year I realise a lot of things about myself. Small things like; I need a dog for my sanity, I am terrible at football, I recoil at the title of *'Miss'*, and my resilience to the word 'faggot' is higher than I expect but never quite high enough. I arrive to class emotionally raw every day. Ready to step into the torrent of chaos and discomfort. I never know what I'm doing and people don't know what I am. The constant pulling at my selvage causes all of my fabric to start to fray; even the true things begin to unravel. Stripped of my strengths, my past identities, I allow myself to uncover a thought that I had buried more than two decades ago, *I think I'm trans.*

I was born trans, I've always been trans, and I am not a woman. *Great, now what?*

School somehow improves. I win over some parents. Colleagues start to ask for my opinion. I become 'Richo' and lose the Miss. I somehow arrange top surgery in a regional hospital and schedule just after my placement ends. I tell my close friends. I tell my mum. I see a doctor about hormones but take nothing until I know I'm in the clear from the prying eyes of parents and children. I tell no one at school for my remaining 18 months.

Why do we always have to talk using this kumbaya shit?

I arrange my grade 10s in a circle. It's the last school week of the year for all of us, but we are restless for different reasons. They sit around me like the edge of a wishing well. The words tumble out. *I'm not going to be a teacher here anymore, I'm finishing early and Friday will be my last day.* I try to hear the sentence land in the soft water of the well I'd created. *I'm going to have surgery, a double mastectomy next week.* I wait for their reactions, and nothing comes. Still no splash. *I'm having this surgery because I am not a woman, and I'm going to start living as a man.* Nothing.

I keep talking to fill the silence. I acknowledge that some of them might not want to be around me anymore. And because they are children I had to say it was ok. It wasn't personal.

It was.

I start to throw the words out of my mouth. Trying to get rid of them, I toss them far away from the false image of me they had spent two years creating. An image of an adult that was funny and smart and reliable. Not some tranny that's lied to them for two years. I couldn't stop myself. I set the expectations so low that by some reasoning, I was so abhorrent that no one should be required to be in the same room as me.

After I finished, some of the students smiled encouragingly. Others looked frightened, or at least hesitant. A group of girls look upset and shocked. I later realised that they thought I had cancer until the last few minutes of my monologue.

Can we go to recess now?

Anticlimactic but it was done. School was out and so was I.

Rowan is a science teacher in lutruwita (Tasmania). He is a mainland import and grew up on Gumbainggir country in NSW before studying and working as a scientist on Yuggera country in Brisbane. Rowan lives with his partner, Ted the dog, and an overgrown garden in nipaluna (Hobart).

image: Jamie James

Carol

she her

It's the love and support and kinship from my queer friends and found family that has sustained and helped me to live and thrive as a queer woman …

JAMIE JAMES

Jamie James is a freelance photographer whose work is informed by the ways people connect, hold memory and culture, and find identity and place. Over the last thirty years James has built an extensive visual archive in collaboration with Australian LGBTIQA+ communities, our First Nations and South Sea Islander Peoples.

Most recently, the State Library of NSW made a comprehensive acquisition of 170 of James's images to their Indigenous Acquisitions Unit, selected from their longitudinal body of social documentary work.

James has freelanced commercially since 1994, specialising in portraiture, health, education and the performing arts, and is a regular contributor to *Bent Street* journal. James will exhibit 30 years from their archive for the Head On International Photo Festival in November 2021, with a working title of "humans being" - a personal selection from 1990-2021.

Jamie's Pronouns are they/them. They live and work in Sydney, Australia, co-parent with Jen, and like dark beer.

http://jamesphoto.com.au/

Dysphoria, My Teacher
JAXSON WEARING

BANG! BANG! Sharp pain shot from my big toe to my heel as I slammed it into the door. I had locked myself into the bathroom after intense emotions flooded my system.

BANG! BANG! Hot tears seared down my face as the rage inside me surged.

BANG! BANG! I screamed out, unable to suppress the fury. It would find its way through me; it would throw itself from every orifice north of my chest where it originated. My heart beat with rage, a primal fury that rendered me helpless. I was someone who had meticulous control over every expression, every word I spoke. Today, however, these emotions turned me into a puppet. I became completely susceptible to its every whim. Rage pulsed through me and every action of mine pulsed with it. I was completely taken over, I had no choice but to become rage.

'Radical acceptance clearly doesn't work for you then,' my counsellor concluded after I recounted this rage attack.

I didn't reply. I was silent as I worked to understand how the concept of radical acceptance could have triggered such violence in me. I had not kicked the bathroom door in since I was a five-year-old. This new moment of uncontrollable emotion had convinced me that I must be seriously unwell. I was at a standstill. Earlier that year I had accepted that I was transgender. I was transgender, but I could not make another move, I could not change. Changing my physical body felt impossible as I did not want to put a synthetic hormone in my body, fearful that I would undo the hard work I had done to heal chronic conditions in my physiology. In truth, I felt brittle, like my system was always on the edge of collapse. The thought of introducing a hormone that could cause deep shifts in my physiology made me feel like I would lose control over my health. Furthermore, the idea of telling the people in my life about my identity was too scary, as the concept of rejection was something that I feverishly avoided. I was so desperate for acceptance I would do anything to avoid being judged or talked about. I would do anything to avoid coming out. It was this standstill that caused my counsellor to introduce the concept of radical acceptance. If I could not change, then I would need to accept myself exactly as I am – a woman in the world. The violence this concept triggered in me made me realise that I could not shut my truth away. It was dysphoria that would bring this fact to my attention through a volcanic display of aggression. Radical acceptance was not a possibility for me. The eruption from within showed me that I would have to change; I would need to find a way to move forward. Dysphoria had crept its way into every crevice of my body, the very crevices that were devoid of my spirit, the crevices that represented the active rejection I practiced of myself daily. It was as though my cells were vehemently trying to tell me that they had had enough and that it was time to change. I simply could not live this way any longer.

This destructive rage was only a fragment of the destruction that I had exerted on myself throughout my life living as female. I was destroying myself by living in self-betrayal. I was living as a version of myself that I felt made everyone else comfortable. The identity I had created as Chloe kept my partner and my family and my patients all chugging along in a sense of security. I was a burden to no-one but myself. I was living in a shell and I let myself stay there, living a false life. In that shell I sought to decimate any chance of my truth expressing itself: I spent long hours at the gym and long hours at work, I restricted eating and I deliberately put myself in situations where I could set myself up to fail. The longer I convinced myself that I was worthless and shameful, the more I could live a life of self-betrayal; serving others only to relieve myself temporarily of the guilt of believing I was damaged. I could not live like this any longer. I had but one choice; to walk myself out of self-destruction.

I was born into a medical system that classified my gender by my anatomy. I was classified as female, one of only two options for classifying sex at birth. The medical system did not have the tools to recognise that I was transgender, and society did not have the consciousness to view me as anything other than female. At birth, I was slapped with an identity label that would define how I was supposed to be raised, what clothes I was supposed to wear, what name I should be given and what roles I should fulfil. These expectations were so far from my truth that the mismatch between my true self and the self I was required to be in this world created a gaping hole. The gaping hole within me was so wide that there was no hope I could bring the two edges together to form a scar and heal. This failure to heal triggered off panic. A seeping wound and its sequelae were a direct threat to my life, there was no solution and there was no answer. This assault on me was remedied with dissociation and my spirit left my physical body to protect itself from the impending pain of death. Only my wound was a concept, it could not be seen. I was alive but I could not live embodied, I was existing in a state of dysphoria.

Dysphoria acted as a protective mechanism. If I connected with my body, I would be triggered into shame by the way my genitals felt and the movement of my breasts. Everyday requirements became triggers. The clothes I wore, the way I spoke, and the touch I received from loved ones poured acid over my internal wounds. I learnt to avoid connection and intimacy to preserve some stability in both my internal and external environment. It was what I needed to stay functional in the world. I felt helpless in the face of the enormity of my lack of connection to myself. My mindset became engulfed with the powerlessness of having been born into the wrong body. I took it on as a belief system and I learnt to identify with only pain and despair. As long as I was numb and disconnected, I could function. I could uphold my relationships at home and in the workplace. It allowed me, in a sense, to move forward without getting swallowed by my gaping wounds. I was walking a very thin line; living an empty life devoid of all connection that was fast becoming as torturous as being inside myself. I was not growing as a person and it was becoming harder and harder to see the purpose of life. I couldn't imagine my life in the future living as a woman. The way I felt was propelling me toward living my life as a man. It was this stark realisation that transition was a necessity, not a choice. I could choose to remain a victim, trapped in dysphoria and dying a soul death; or I could find it in me to choose life instead. Rather than resist, I accepted that the mismatch I felt in my body was telling me to transition. Transitioning became an act of self-love, a celebration of me and the acknowledgement of my own authenticity and human right to express it. In doing this, I faced the dysphoria. I left the protection dysphoria had given me behind and I embraced its presence in my body.

The day I took testosterone for the first time my existence changed. Everything that I had experienced and everything that I had known flipped in a millisecond. I entered my body in a rush, like a truck hitting me. All at once, I felt what it was like to be alive and inside my body. Brand new biochemistry was forming, and it created an orchestra of sound and light that reverberated through every cell. There was now something within my physicality that my spirit could attach to. I felt myself descend from a place outside myself and into my body. I flowed down through my arms and into my fingers like pulling sleeves of a jumper over my shoulders. I wiggled my toes and I allowed myself to breathe with the density of my body. The gaping wound within purged its contents and sealed itself in front of my eyes. The crevices that had been filled with shame cleared as the light of my spirit flowed through them. I had come into my body. My system could now vibrate with the energy of my soul. I was home.

Now I was in my body, I was no longer protected from the mismatch between my true self and the self I had forced myself to live by. I felt, with full force, the total rejection of how I had experienced my female body and feminine aspects until now. The very impact of my spirit entering my body blew away the coping mechanisms I had used to numb the pain and exist in the world. I became extremely vulnerable. I could feel everything. My psyche began to process past experiences I had not been able to fully experience, like my first day at school and that time my mother put me in a dress for family photos. I had a moment of clarity where I could see how dysphoria had thread its way through my life since my first memory at four years old. I became keenly aware of how certain behaviours and thought processes, down to the underwear I selected in the morning, was influenced by the mismatch of gender. I had outrun the race. There was nothing to run from anymore. Rather than run from myself, I met myself exactly where I was at.

In this state of surrender I experienced dysphoria in a whole new way. It could not protect me from knowing the truth about my gender. My journey was shifting now from trying to live as a woman to discovering just what it meant to be authentic. I felt small and powerless in the face of change. My pre-transition self could no longer exist in the new reality I was creating. In this new reality, there was no place for self-destruction. I needed to be held in this pause; only care and nurturing would soothe the rawness. It was just me now, a small pea in an adult shell. I had to give myself space to grow. I had to trust that I would grow into the truest part of me. I learnt to treat myself like a child, with patience and compassion. After all the attempted self-destruction in the years prior, I owed it to myself to find out who I really was and allow that essence to come through.

As I grew as a person, dysphoria moved from within me to around me. It was not something I could avoid or suppress; it never went away. Eventually I stopped trying to resist it and opened to new ways of feeling and seeing. I wanted to transform myself and refused to become a slave to the constant pain and shame. I felt it was trying to tell me something. As I listened more, and processed the triggers that caused it to flare, dysphoria developed a voice. It spoke when I acted in ways that were not true to myself. Dysphoria became a barometer for self-betrayal. By doing so, dysphoria showed me where honesty lay.

I had been on testosterone for one year when I started wanting everyone to recognise the man I had become. I had become rigid and frustrated in the face of constant misgendering and misnaming. I started to believe that people could not recognise my gender because I was not male enough. My behaviour changed as I sought to act in a 'male' way: I talked less, and I used fewer mannerisms when I spoke. I tried to be more stoic and show fewer emotions. I even refrained from showing affection with my partner in public. I shunned the more feminine parts of me: my intuition, my capacity to nurture and my softness. However, the frustration only increased as the misgendering continued. In my quest to become inarguably male, the dysphoria dialled up. I felt shame seep through the crevices that had begun to heal over the past year.

Dysphoria came to me and said *you are repressing your true self.*

I rebutted, why couldn't people see me as a man?

It spoke back, soothingly *people will see you how they want to see you.* Then, I understood.

I could not continue to shape my identity around how I wanted to be seen. I needed to discover my identity and express it no matter what that looked like to others. Only by mastering this could I live a life free of the traps of what other people thought of me. Dysphoria showed me where I was repressing authentic parts of myself. Regardless of whether they were viewed as feminine or not, they were still true parts of me. Dysphoria became not just a vehicle for highlighting the mismatch between my gender and my sex assigned at birth, but it had also become a gauge for where I was moving further away from my own truth. When I listened to dysphoria, say I was repressing myself in the name of presenting as more masculine, I realised that I had bought into societal rules around gender. I found my true path, outside of the gender norms of society. Dysphoria showed me the way to becoming whole.

Dysphoria revealed the parts of me that were disembodied. In doing so, it became my guide, highlighting the areas within me that were mismatched. When I lived as a woman, it protected me from the pain of separation. As I began my transition, it met me at my new level of bravery and pulled back the veil. Behind the veil was a void and within that void was pain, but with the pain was also a fragment of me. Dysphoria became the light in the darkness. These fragments were pieces of a puzzle that, once seen and understood, I could integrate, heal and reclaim my true self. The truth is that I had not been born in the wrong body; I had been born into the perfect body for my life. I had been born into a body that would only settle for the truest version of me and would not stop talking until I saw and accepted that. My life changed as I changed. I learnt to thrive through connection with myself and others. I reclaimed my anatomy from the clutches of an outdated medical system. By accepting my physicality, I was gifted the empowerment I would need to change it – not with guilt, but with grace. I could reclaim my past, present and future. Over time, dysphoria showed me the way back to myself. Dysphoria wasn't a condition nor a disorder but one of my very greatest teachers.

Jaxson Wearing is a transgender man from Sydney, Australia. He is a holistic healthcare practitioner who runs a health and wellness centre in Sydney. He is also an educator having taught anatomy and physiology at university for over ten years. As an author he tells his story of transformation and personal growth in an effort to inspire others to do the same.

Waves
NATE McCARTHY

Before the virus, there had been the fires, a whole summer of dark skies and dread. Scott checked the bushfire update map as soon as he woke each morning, not bothering to open the curtains to another shrouded day. There wasn't enough room on the fire service map for all the flame icons. They stacked up like bad clip art, vying for land.

The sky was dead and his work felt ridiculous. Each of the gardens he worked on in Sydney went into a state of shock and decline. He cleared gutters of ashen leaves that had blown in from somewhere worse off than the inner city and mulched everything he could. Lawns were the husks of foolish ideas. Weeds were a distant luxury and watering was out of the question. In desperation he got a job pruning huge old street trees that were dying after a vicious string of 49 degree days. He breathed sawdust and smoke as the year ended and worried about leaving any petrol tool in his van for more than a few minutes in the heat. Combustibles felt like sin. Who knew what could happen in this heat.

By the year's end he couldn't work another day in the thick smoke and quit after he puked on his chainsaw halfway up a Camphor laurel. He waited out the rest of the summer in his room with a portable air conditioner running constantly. The smell of burnt eucalyptus got in his hair and his clothes and in the wet sheets he hung up to block out the western sun from his flat. The coast was a horror show. Footage of people huddling in the dark on piers ready to submerge in the sea while the fire bore down on them entered his dreams. Everyone he knew outside of the inner city was under threat. Scott started to get drunk at home during the day, scuttling out for a bag of party ice and groceries before 8am and settling in til the next morning. Like everybody else, he tried to breathe as little air from outside as possible.

After a short reprieve of smokeless days and autumn cool when the fires were all finally out, everybody was ordered inside. Scott was able to go to work in the gardens he'd looked after before. They had recovered from the summer scorch, and had covered up their wounds in green. The work was a gift. Clients waved from indoors when he arrived with his tools and left his cash outside for him in crumpled envelopes. He weeded alone in sloping backyards by the urban stink of the Cook's River and watched the stream of locked-down people walk by on their permitted exercise hour. He worked close to the back fence line to be in smiling and nodding range.

Most evenings, Scott renovated his van as a project to keep him more or less sober and hopeful. He built a raised bed with slide-out storage and took a whole week to install wood panelling on the walls and floor. Without hesitation he traded his most valuable indoor plants with an electrician to install soft uplighting in each corner. His little cabin on wheels made him feel so happy that he shook. The big bed with his good linen and feather quilt on it helped him shed his worries about ending the lease on his flat. A single bed would have been more practical. But a person could hope. He was packed up and ready the weekend before lockdown ended.

The night before he left, Scott drove his new home around his neighbourhood to check if anything jiggled or clanged. Misery was a dirt road and a poorly packed pantry. The streets were empty and dark as lunged over speed humps and turned circles in cul-de-sac. Everything was stowed snugly in the van; his chainsaw, his books, his kitchen things. He rounded a corner back onto the main street and passed a slow convoy of the public order and riot squad in three white Nissan Patrols. 'Fuckity fuck,' he blurted, out of habit. He really needed to get his license updated. But the big men ignored him. They passed slowly like sharks into other quiet waters.

And so the very first day it was permitted, Scott drove his van south down the coast, aiming for a string of beaches halfway to the Victorian border. He left before dawn and was on the other side of Wollongong before he knew it. All lockdown, he'd imagined this – his foot on the accelerator and clear morning light falling on his lap. The sea was calm beside the highway and the steep rocky shoreline stretched into the distance. Now in the free morning he smiled. He had been desperate to leave Sydney for a long time. Paddocks were green and coral trees flowered on hills. You could forget the summer if you wanted to. It didn't seem right but it was a relief. With steadier hands than he'd had in ages, he poured himself a coffee from his thermos without slowing down. The air was clean and the day was

cool, and Covid hadn't washed over the country in the wave they'd
first feared. It was unbelievable. He was on a big, wide, lark.

Scott pulled into a small town for a piss and an egg and bacon roll
just before Kiama. Men's bathrooms still felt strange to him. The
separation of weeing and pooing, and the use of public foyer space
for communal pissing always jarred a little. Troughs were for animals.
He'd thought that ever since nipping into the boys toilets to retrieve a
footy in second grade.

Boys have two places to go, his best friend Mike explained at
lunchtime. *Troughs for wee, dunnies for poo.*

You pee in front of each other? Scott had asked. *Like, you see each other's
willies?*

You're not 'sposed to look, Mike said.

Strange, but, Scott mumbled

Spose it is, Mike said, sucking his blackcurrant juice up with a
straw.

In a few hours he would stop at his favourite headland where you
could drive the van right into a grassy thicket behind a long sweep of
beach. Barely anybody went there and the nights were quiet and starlit
– there was never the threat of being woken and forced to drive on by
a ranger. There were, of course, other threats. But it felt right. It was
the place where he had spoken out loud the things he most wanted :
an ease with knots, a crowded table, a voice that matched his hands.

He cried on and off while he drove through to Moruya. The bush
wasn't completely razed now, for months had passed. But what had
been a thick forest by the highway was now like a strange cash crop
with one type of tree and no understory. The spotted gums that had
survived by the highway were skeletal and black and beginning to be
flushed with stress shoots. A lush decline. He wasn't above reading
himself in the landscape. People could put out showy growth like
crazy when they were all but burned up, he thought. And what was he
doing, taking off at a time like this? Doubt spiralled out of him in
widening arcs until he made himself remember the shut-up rooms of
his flat, the malaise of smoke, the stockpiling of toilet paper and the
endless waiting. There were worse things than being lost and knowing
it.

The sun was still high when he got to the beach and nosed his van
into the little clearing in the bush right at the mouth of the lagoon
that was just closed to the sea. There were no other vehicles, just one

woman walking a dog far up the other end. The shallows of the lagoon water were thick with ash. On the beach, the tide line was a twist of burnt sticks and seaweed and charcoal. It horrified him. Still, if the tide had to hold everything together, the old ashes and new seaweed, then so could he.

Night came quickly and he warmed up chickpea curry on a gas burner and slopped it with yoghurt and lime pickle. He lay on his bed in the van and scratched his beard and listened to the wetland. For a while he was peaceful. And then, in another moment, only pretending quite hard to be. He was so far from anyone and he was afraid. He locked himself in the van and closed the curtains. The cold lump of the metal baseball bat under his bedspread felt good alongside him. Barely room to swing it in the van.

If people – men – come, they'll come in cars and I'll see the headlights from way off, he thought. Nobody had watched him drive in or even knew he was there. Besides, even if they had, they wouldn't have seen anyone they'd get an idea about hurting. But his fear remained. It had never lightened when his body changed, nor did he ever expected it to. The dark was still the dark. And there was always a man out there, waiting. Even if that man wasn't interested in him anymore.

Waves crashed, birds screeched their night calls, and no footsteps crunched up to the van, even with his mind twitchy and prone to hearing a huge man where only a possum hopped. He put his headphones in and fell asleep to Raymond Carver reading a grim short story about a man drinking alone in his kitchen. But the night was cold and he woke to piss often. He relieved himself expertly into a jar in the dark, judged its remaining capacity by the rising pitch of his gurgling urine. In the morning he lay in his warm bed with the curtains open to the bush and felt still and calm. The terrors of the night were over and he could have months ahead of him like this. Scott didn't dwell on what would happen if the state went into lockdown again and he was on the wind in a pandemic. Running away, running towards, outrunning. It didn't matter now.

Scott had breakfast at the lagoon's edge. Fresh coffee made him brilliant and sharp like he'd done a line. He read while he boiled eggs and watched a heron on the far bank as he turned a page. And then, with his chainsaw and trowel stowed under his bed, and the newly-raised dole pooling in his bank account, he slipped out of his clothes and ran past the charcoal tideline to the ocean. Scott screamed as he plunged through the first wave. Though he couldn't stand the cold a second longer he swam out and was lifted over the next swell. He had to. Because the sun could cloud over any moment, and because it was better to swim out and meet what was coming than to wait and see where it would break.

Nate McCarthy lives on the South Coast of NSW on Yuin Country. They grow garlic and have a dog which is roughly the same size as a BBQ chicken.

The Right Fit
THEO DUNNE

'She's a girl,' Jonathan says. 'Pick her to go first.'

I look at Tom. I shrug with one hand and spin the ball in the other. Jonathan's older, taller. He's ten. We're seven. But it doesn't matter who goes first, I'm still going to win.

'Yeah but she's like a boy,' Tom says. I smile and square up behind the invisible line between the bin and the verandah post.

Jonathan eyes my basketball shorts and baggy, tattered t-shirt and frowns. 'So, you want to be a boy?'

I stand up straight again. The last light of the day is sinking behind the shed and the basketball ring is getting harder and harder to see. We've only got a few precious minutes until it disappears.

'Yeah, I guess so. So what?'

Jonathan shakes his head. 'But you're not a boy,' he says. 'Like when you go to the toilets, do you go to the boy's or the girl's?'

I look down at the ball and rub my hand over the worn away Spalding label. 'The girls,' I say, in a quiet voice.

Tom shifts uncomfortably but says nothing. Jonathan smirks, nods once, then bends down into a sloppy defensive stance – as if the argument is over, as if he's already won.

The sun is gone and a chill pervades the air. My jaw clenches. 'Whatever, I don't care,' I say, spitting the words out like apple seeds.

I shoot the ball, pushing upwards as hard as I can. It misses.

The summer before high school, I stand in the change room of the uniform shop holding a heavy woollen skirt, while Gavin DeGraw's I Don't Want to Be plays from a football-shaped CD player in the corner. There's no air conditioning and the Adelaide heat weighs in from all sides. I step into the skirt, it's long and itchy, like a blanket smothering my body. I can't get the button to do up.

'How are you going?' Mum asks.

'It's too tight.'

'Remember, it's supposed to go on your waist, not your hips,' she says.

I pull it up around my waist, do the button up and then try to tug it down. The fabric clutches against my hips, unmoving, the button digging into my hip bone. 'It feels wrong.'

'I know, but don't worry, high waists will be back in fashion one day.'

'No, they won't,' I grumble.

I huff and yank the button out of its loop, then pull the skirt off. I glare at the mirror. Pools of fat have materialised overnight on my hips and chest. The sight makes my stomach churn. Puberty feels molten inside me, hot and gooey. Unstoppable. I pull my Rusty t-shirt back on. It's the same t-shirt I've worn almost every day this summer, but I can't unsee the lumps. The bulges. The way my t-shirt pulls tightly over my hips. I feel nauseous.

My body has changed too much and now nothing fits right.

The walk to my new school takes around five songs. My iPod Nano jangles in my dress pocket, along with a pack of chewies, Papaw lip balm and loose change for a rainbow Paddle Pop. Sometimes, Jake walks to school with me. He's in my year and his bus stop is close to my house. I squash down jealousy as I stare at his uniform, a combination of navy shorts and white shirt, while I wear a blue checked dress that ruffles and lifts in the wind. I feel exposed, despite the shorts I wear underneath.

When we get to school, Jake goes right, to the boy's toilets, the unknowable land of urinals. I go left around the old chapel and into the labyrinth of teenage girlhood. I don't see him again until lunch time, when the boys play football and the girls sit around the oval in circles. I sit with the girls. I watch them, studying the role and practicing the lines. I learn to talk about The O.C. with sweeping hand gestures and the flick of a side fringe. I create a vexing costume of mascara, tinted moisturiser and enough Impulse spray to ensure the synthetic flower scent lingers in my throat and clothes until I get home.

I avoid mirrors. We go to the bathroom in groups and when I'm looking away from my reflection, I notice how the other girls look at theirs. How they adjust their collars and buttons, tug on seams and sleeves. Some have even altered their dresses altogether: raised the hemlines and cinched the waists. Maybe it's an issue for all girls, maybe our uniforms just aren't designed to fit right.

I test my performance of teenage girlhood on a new audience when I play basketball for a club outside of school. My team huddles around in red hoodies, talking about their favourite characters from The O.C., while waiting for practice to start. I follow along with interest but then the topic changes to boys. I freeze. I hate this part of the act the most. I look away until the conversation moves on and notice one of the girls, Emma, is watching me. There's a glint in her eye and the hint of a smile. My heart thuds. Does she know? Can she tell that my clothes, my words, are all an act?

That night, Emma messages me online and we chat for hours. Then the same thing happens the next night and the next. It becomes habitual. Each night after dinner, I go online, Emma initiates a chat and we talk until the early hours of the morning. She tells me about her day, her school and her friends. I ask questions to keep the conversation going. When we say goodnight it's with a multitude of x's and o's. It fills my chest with a pleasant burn, like taking a big gulp of a fizzy drink.

The short nights slip into long school days and into sleepy afternoons.

I sit at the kitchen bench, rocking back on a stool and eating a Pizza Pocket. My sister and her friend are getting ready for the school formal, putting on their dresses with a surge of excitement. My sister's dress is silky and pale pink. Seamless. She's dabbing foundation on her calf, on a white patch where the dog had licked off her fake tan.

Her friend looks at me. Her eyes drop down to my threadbare grey t-shirt with its worn-off Adidas logo and holes. It's my favourite t-shirt, loose and soft, and I change into it as soon as I get home from school. She doesn't say anything, there's only a slight crease between her brows, but I've become an expert on this look: disapproval. My skin itches even after her eyes have flicked away. She pokes my sister in the ribs and mutters something about her date. They giggle and whisper, but I can't hear what they're saying.

Grandma ambles over to me. She clutches a disposable camera in one hand and pats my shoulder with the other. 'Don't worry. It'll be your turn soon.'

I grimace. I try to picture myself in the flowy pink dress. I picture a date but can only see the vague shape of a boy – tall, broad, in a sleek James Bond suit. I try to picture myself next to the boy, in the dress, his arm around me. Dread burrows into my skin like a burning infection.

It's only 5:00 pm and I'm already exhausted. I excuse myself to my room, but before I do, I ask Mum if I can get some new clothes.

The basketball season flies by and our team wins more games than not. Emma and I continue to chat online each night. She talks about parties and drinking and kissing boys, and I say things I think a girl would say. We start hanging out in person after games and it becomes a patchwork of hidden glances, long hugs, and sleepovers that last for a week. My chest aches when I'm around her. It aches more when I'm not.

Late one night, around 2:00 am, my eyes itching with tiredness, I write: 'I wish I could be a boy so I could grow tall enough to dunk the ball.'

Emma replies, 'I wish I was a boy, so we could fall in love and get married.'

I type out, 'I'll be the boy.' But I don't press send.

When I finally get into bed my head is reeling.

The next weekend, Emma and I stroll into the movie theatre and hand our She's the Man ticket stubs to a teenage boy with a maroon vest. The smell of rain sticks to me. My toes are wet and cold in my thongs, my only footwear that are neither 'boy' nor 'girl'.

'I'm gonna go to the bathroom before we go in,' Emma says.

I go to follow her but then slow my pace as I see boys waiting outside the door, waiting for their dates. I decide to wait too. But the sips of Sprite swell in my bladder. I last a minute before I break and push open the bathroom door.

The movie starts. Her arm rests next to mine, our elbows touching. Our bodies angle towards each other and my neck aches in this awkward position. I don't move. At one point, her hand shifts fractionally closer but then the credits roll, and she pulls her hand away. I wrench my neck upright. For the entire drive home there's a persistent niggle in the base of my skull.

Summer comes and goes, and the basketball season starts again. Emma is on a different team. We don't talk much anymore but I still sit at the computer for hours and watch the space where her name isn't. I get more sleep now that I'm not chatting online until late, but somehow, I'm even more tired. Basketball becomes exhausting. So I quit.

School feels different too. Boys talk in deeper, louder voices. Girls talk in whispers and rising inflections. I hold my breath when I go to my locker, so I don't gag on Lynx body spray and lewd comments.

I grew taller over the holiday break. It's only two centimetres but it's made grabbing rebounds easier. I tell Jake that I've grown, he looks at my chest. 'I can see that.'

I shove his shoulder. 'Piss off.' My face feels hot and prickly.

He laughs and puts his hands up, acquiescing. 'Calm down, it's just a joke.'

That weekend, at a party, I sink into a cracked leather couch, my skin buzzing. The room smells of weed, sugary drinks and vomit. The music is loud, but I don't recognise the songs. The couch dips as a boy sits next to me. I can't remember his name, but he's nice, undemanding. When he kisses me, I let him, but it doesn't feel real; it's like I'm watching it happen to someone else through a TV screen.

I graduate from a girl to a woman unceremoniously in my first fulltime job.

'What should the kids call you, Miss …?'

It makes my skin prickle every time.

The job is in a regional town. The landscape is beautiful and a sprawling contradiction: it's urban but outback, desert but with sea and mountains. I live in a small two-bedroom unit and fall asleep to the rumble of freight trains and gurgle of pipes. The yard, like most of the town, is barren. A dirt patch with a strip of fake grass. A girl I meet at work, Sophie, offers to help me plant some veggies. I accept, even though it seems futile. Only the hardiest of shrubs seem to survive here. I had even witnessed a real-life tumble weed bouncing down the road.

One day after work, I get ambushed by curly brown hair and facts about gardening. Sophie digs into the red clay with her bare hands and gouges tiny holes for the sweet potato seedlings to go in. She's so tenacious, I'm surprised when impatient digging becomes gentle coaxing, as she eases the seedlings from their containers. Her hands are gentle but unwavering. I watch, my gaze unwavering too.

It's both freeing and lonely living on my own in a new town. I buy men's clothes online and when they arrive, I close all the curtains before trying them on. I pull on the jeans and my stomach sinks. They don't hang loose like they had on the model, instead they cling to my thighs and accentuate the dip and protrusion of my hips. I put my high-waisted women's jeans back on. I try on the t-shirt, the seams are straight and rigid, too narrow for my hips and too loose for my shoulders. I grit my teeth and fling the clothes into the corner of my bedroom.

The same week, a kid taps my leg at work, I bend down to her level and she looks at me for a long moment. 'You look like a boy.'

The adults in the room turn with gaping mouths. Before they can correct her, I give her a smile and shrug.

The sweet potatoes grow. Sophie comes over to help me dig them out and we roast them and make dinner together. We talk for hours, sitting at the dark wooden round table that once belonged to my Grandma. She tells me about her brother and father, how she's only been back to Queensland twice in four years. There's a sadness there but I don't pry. We all have our secrets, but the omission feels profound for someone usually so upfront, someone who never hesitates to ask for what she wants.

She asks me to add more salt to the potatoes.

She asks me to be her girlfriend.

I say yes, feeling sure in a way I never have before. But there's still an ache in my chest, a disconnect, like a button hanging from a sweater.

We sit on the couch side-by-side while two fuzzy dogs at our feet grizzle in their sleep. I'm looking through Goodreads when I see a book I recognise – I remember the cover, the red shoes next to an oily rainbow on a wet road. I had picked it up once at a bookstore, flicked through its pages. It's a story of a girl who becomes a boy. I read the comment section and after clicking on a few links, I end up on Instagram, scrolling through the hashtag: #transgender. There's an avalanche of posts. So many people. So many backwards chronologies of flexed biceps, chest scars and testosterone vials. My heart pounds.

I try to tell myself that it's not really a possibility, not for me, but it doesn't work. I lie in bed tossing and turning. Uncomfortable. Woman is now a bed too rigid to sleep in.

Soon after, when Sophie and I are driving back from the city, a long and tedious journey, I confess I might be trans. She's not surprised, just smiles and nods. 'Do you wanna talk about it?'

I do. I talk and talk until my vocal cords are sore and bruised and the landscape has shifted from city buildings to open countryside. My anxieties race alongside the car, going 110km per hour, but inside, there's a stillness, like the feeling of driving onto a paved road after kilometres of gravel.

That night, I buy the book.

Two years later, when my skin is greasier, my voice deeper and my hair shorter, I push open the door to the men's toilets for the first time. It looks the same as the women's, cold and sterile, except with the addition of a urinal. It doesn't feel momentous like I thought it would. It just feels ordinary. And if anything, the two doors, two options, feels too restrictive.

I pee as quickly as I can and hurry back outside where Sophie is waiting. She's trying not to squeal with excitement. We walk out of the shopping centre and into the warm Queensland air. It smells like fresh bread, tropical fruits and flowers. My phone vibrates and I smile. It's a message from a friend, congratulating me on officially changing my name. My skin tingles with the thrill that I no longer have to hide. I tuck my phone into the pocket of my men's boardies and smooth down my navy men's t-shirt – it's my favourite outfit and while the clothes cling slightly to my hips, I don't care. I'm comfortable.

I drive us home, one hand on the wheel, the other entwined with Sophie's hand. There's a congruous hum as Bryan Adams' 'Summer of '69' plays on the radio. The buzzing anticipation of hot, humid months drifts in through the open windows.

Maybe my clothes will never fit perfectly. But maybe what matters is finding something that feels right.

Theo Dunne is a transmasc writer who lives and works on Turrbal and Yuggera land. His work has also been published in *Dubnium and Kill Your Darlings.*

'I Will Myself'
ELWIN SCHOK

Tensions in Perception and Information for Transmasc Individuals beginning HRT

1. Scientific account

Abstract

This is my fourth start trying to write this. I keep beginning and then putting a page break and beginning again. In this current word document (that is, when this is first being written), there are three draft-starts stopped midsentence and two abandoned plans on the following pages.

Introduction

Every account I hear of people accessing hormones seems different (see for e.g. Jacques 2008; Preciado 2008; Sullivan, Martin Ed., et al 2019).[1]

Methodology

I have joined several facebook groups over the past 6 months: 'genderqueer pride & allies & friends'; 'trans support club narrm'; 'nonbinary transition'.[2] I have made a spreadsheet on my computer. I search for posts about HRT, more specifically about testosterone.[3] I log them in my spreadsheet. I have different parameters I code them

---

[1] I am aware of the limitations of this source list for my argument, given the highly localised and temporal aspects of HRT access and given that each of the listed accounts is from a different place and time. While perhaps there are more local and specific sources that would potentially amount to a contradiction of what I am saying through yielding a more cohesive picture, I couldn't be bothered doing any actual research and so have just listed the books I have read in the last 6 months that include a person's account of accessing HRT. Also maybe there just aren't a lot of more local and specific sources? I don't know!

[2] pseudonyms used to preserve anonymity

[3] it is 3am and a jagged buzz hums through me. every comment I read aches my chest. *need sleep* but can't. my body feels like it's floating/glowing/*something*. it is hard to describe exactly what this reading means to me

for: positive and negative affect;[4] increased or decreased dosage since beginning—things like that.

Results

In my sample, 67% of people increase dosage after beginning and 15% had stopped completely at the time of posting; 59% of results are coded as positive affect (see Fig. 1); 80% of posters have been taking HRT for less than a year.[5]

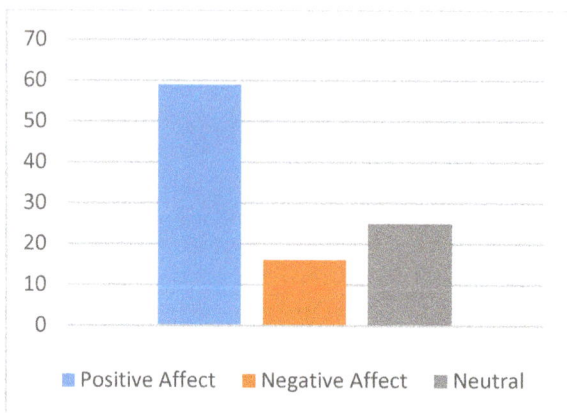

Fig. 1 Affect in fb comments mentioning testosterone

Discussion

The fact that each doctor tells me a slightly different thing about starting T feels unmanageably unstable (Fuckthis 2021).

2. Elucidation through relationship

What is the narrative voice of this piece? I had this vision that this entire piece would be through the perspective of a kind of friend—or lover. But the initial section wrote itself in a kind of glitchy first person. I end up feeling kind of naff (?) writing about a projected self

---

[4] affect was coded based off the use of evaluative predicates such as *horrible, ideal,* and *nasty,* or affective predicates such as *glad, so glad,* or *amazed.* Each predicate used was given either a positive score between +1 and +3 or a negative score between -1 and -3. A comment was coded as neutral in the absence of these predicates or if the total score was equal to zero

[5] these results are fabricated for artistic effect, informed by the vague impression I have gleaned through compulsive consumption of comments

from another's perspective. It feels somehow nakeder than first-person autobiography. I don't know how to stop being desperately self-conscious.

An attempt:

Okay so! I am a friend/lover! And there is this person who is my friend/lover!

And they are SUPER hot like I just want to bang them all the time because they are so hot and cool and awesome.

Great, this section is done. perfect.

3. Glimpses from others

The draft-starts (still below, as I am writing this—I am not yet confident enough in this current draft to delete them) tried more widely to interrogate or embody the perspectives of a variety of other people to give a fuller account. But I just don't really know if I can do that right now?[6] I am bleeding again this month and currently have five separate light sources on in my room: two glass-shaded ceiling bulbs, the glare of the screen, the pink glow of my diffuser, a tiny black desk lamp. I thought the layering of light would make me feel safe, but instead, the way that each light illuminates its own fractured world overwhelms me: as if I need to hold on to my singular perspective to stop everything from splitting apart.

There is something that feels insistent though about stepping outside the self, like, something that I can't communicate from my interiority

For example:

a primary school friend told me she had seen a photo of them[7] in her feed. She had stared at the features of this person, this person she hadn't seen for over 10 years, trying to find the child in them. She had this kind of sense of what they looked like as a child, even though she couldn't actually picture it in her mind. Perhaps a straight nose and pursed mouth? Kind of tangled dark hair? Short? But it was more a feeling than an image, her memory of what they had looked like. She had spent several minutes paused on the picture, playing a kind of game of perception. First, she would look at the face as if it were a stranger on the street.

---

[6] pressure on the goop in my skull; forehead buzz; thoughts corroding before fully formed

[7] these examples contain third party experiences of me from the perspective of the friend/lover from Section 2. A fracturing of perspective—seeing self through double mirror

Then look at the face with the whole history of the face in mind. Stranger face. History face. Stranger face. History face. She told me that she had laughed, later, to two mutual friends she had brunch with every couple of months, that it was so shocking how clearly she could find the child in the face, even though she would have never recognised them if they had come into her shop, looking for a desk lamp, for example.

or:

I spoke to one of their clients once. He asked me how long I had known them for and then went on to say that he would have never guessed really. Not that he had a problem with it or anything. If I thought that was what he was saying. No not at all. He just yeah, wouldn't have guessed.

or:

after they died, I tucked myself into their bed. I reached for the testogel bottle on the dresser and, seized by a sudden impulse, squirted a dollop onto the back of my hand. Cold and smelled like vodka. I wondered if it would do anything to me, picturing a sudden moustache erupting on my top lip. I looked in the mirror. The hair still fine and sparse. Good. Then I ripped into a pack of pringles they had stuffed behind their headboard, the tang of BBQ seasoning hitting my tongue. Their facebook account was still logged in on my phone and all day I had been getting notifications for posts mourning their death: 'I'll miss you'/ 'you are the best person in the world'/ 'you are truly the hottest person I have ever laid eyes on— gosh you're an adonis'/ 'I am so sad we will never get to fuck—it has been my dream to suck your cock for many years'. I ate every pringle in the pack and then pulled the doona up so it covered my face.

or:[8]

4. Conclusion

4.1 the ache in my chest is metal filings magnetised towards my sternum

The fact that positive affect was artistically fabricated by the author at over three times the rate of negative affect demonstrates that posters in trans facebook groups mostly have positive experiences of HRT and/or the author is mostly paying attention to positive experiences of HRT. The author is now the expert on trans people's (/their own) affective stance towards HRT.

---

[8] Two months on T, there are no models exactly for the me I feel myself to be. I have had a whole life of being conditioned to picture a future in which I don't exist

4.2 piece together what could happen from the narratives of others

posted progress pics illustrating variations on the clinic's printed
timeline. shared appointment notes in comments. another's
experience delivering possibilities left behind in waiting rooms

4.3. suggestions for further study

through writing it, I will myself into a future of being perceived as
masculine
    through writing it, I will myself into a future of sharing knowledge
    through writing it, I will myself

Elwin Schok is a writer, performer and linguist who works across artistic and
academic mediums. Their writing engages with language and the body. They can be
found on Twitter at @ElwinSchok.

AT LEAST 3
WEEKS. I
WATCH AS
BROWN
CREEPS
THROUGH
BANANA,
TURNING
IT SPOT-
TED AND
RANCID,
EVENTU-
ALLY
LEAVING
NOTHING
BUT MUSH.
I WATCH AS
GRAPES
GROW
SOGGY

Static
MADDOX GIFFORD

I've taken to staring at shoes. On the tram, mostly, when the crush of bodies has me trapped in place, body a rigid mast and one arm locked to the nearest pole with a brittle grip. Eye contact is the bane of my existence, and my diminutive size places my natural line of sight at chest height with the average person – too awkward – so I keep my gaze fixed firmly to the floor, roaming over the shoes of strangers. Within minutes an ache will spread down the back of my neck from the strain; my arm will begin to tremble; my back, bent inwards in a forced hunch, will emit a steady throb of familiar pain. The most dissonant and jarring of my favourite songs will be blasting through my headphones in an attempt to transform the sensory overload to one of sound. To disrupt the relentless static drone of inhabiting a body.

It is never more than partially successful. I am constantly, fiercely, aware of my body. The claustrophobic conditions of CBD traffic represent the worst of it, but the ache is constant, like the ticking of a clock on the wall that, once noticed, refuses to be ignored. Discomfort. Dysphoria. The latter, an uninvited third party in my every interaction. Dysphoria hears me gushing or giggling, senses the excitement vibrating in my bones, and brusquely reminds me that I am not allowed this. That if I would only sacrifice every scrap of softness within me, I might stand a chance at passing; might go one day without hearing that painful "Excuse me, miss?" I don't truly believe it. But the pitch of my eager voice makes me flinch, so I shrink back down inside of myself anyway.

> The upside of mental illness is that it gives you a lot of inspiration hey

Text Message

I stare at the message until my eyes begin to water for lack of blinking. My eventual response is as cutting as my distaste for confrontation will allow. No, is the gist of it. Actually, no, depression stole my joy of writing for years and I haven't yet been able to complete a piece this year without a messy combination of at least three of the following; weed, uppers, alcohol, coffee. Verbal self-abuse bitten out at a low enough volume to keep the words from carrying to my neighbours through the thin walls.

I feel bad for snapping. He's experienced depression as well – has told me about it. Year 12 was the catalyst: hardly a rare phenomenon among the HSC veterans who, if I had been able to hack it, would have been my peers. Mine, though, first struck in Year 8 and has since shown no signs of ever truly abating. I find myself feeling a pathetic sense of superiority over this, as though my word on the matter means more because of it, and justifies my reaction. As though I know best. The Expert. His depression came and passed, and mine lurks under the surface leaking poison, striking at any given moment. My brain is potentially more fucked up than his. Well la-dee-da.

Two-minute noodles are a depressed person's best friend – a depressed writer especially. I'm partial to the Maggi type, mi goreng, purple-and-black packaging. I have consumed hundreds of these packets of noodles, and for some reason I baulk at the thought of eating any other kind. The familiar ritual of their preparation soothes me.

Boil the water. Tear a thin strip down the flimsy plastic. Set the flavour sachets aside, to be flattened along one edge by firm thumbnails. Watch the noodles soften and separate in the churning saucepan. Drain. Pour. Add the flavour sachets, and extra sweet soy sauce, and enough sriracha to make my eyes water. Mix thoroughly.

Every bowl is the same. Simple, predictable, a uniform texture throughout. An intense, overwhelming flavour. A thick warmth coating the inside of my mouth. This is often the only meal I can manage on uppers or psychedelics. It's somehow comforting to know that, in sickness or in health, exhausted or hyper, drunk or high or gurning – no matter what jokes my body may play on me, some things I can handle.

I come across an article in the *New York Times* that warns of the dangers of chest-binding, citing "symptoms like back and chest pain, overheating and shortness of breath". Peppered throughout are quotes: some from 'concerned parents', a few from doctors, and several from organisations I have never heard of – one of which, the rabbithole of the comments section suggests, may not actually exist. There is a single quote from a trans person: a 17-year-old boy who once spent months binding day and night, far surpassing the recommended limit of eight hours. No other trans perspectives are included.

When my indignation at that imbalance has begun to fade, the predominant emotion I am left with is amusement. This all-too-serious *Breaking News! Read all about it!* Hot Take feels as lukewarm as a forgotten cup of tea.

Yes, I am aware of the back pain, and the sweating, and the panting after a single flight of stairs. It's old news. I can't think of a single trans person who would be surprised by the information. This article, rather, is for those who know us. For our relatives, mostly: another exaggerated tidbit to be brandished during the Interrogation that inevitably occurs sometime after the Coming Out. A vehicle for disgust or disapproval, disguised as concern.

It bothers me that the author, who appears to be a cisgender woman, focuses so closely on the physicality of binding but neglects to explore what it *feels* like. She has no way of knowing, of course. She knows logically what it does, and why. But how am I to explain the curious sensation of being smothered so firmly it feels like a hug, the kind that steals your breath for its duration but fills you with joy? The comfort of being safe, hidden away under as many layers as raw, reactive nerves will allow, pressed flat like moist tofu between unread books? Sometimes it feels like a binder is the only thing keeping all of me inside this body. Surely without it my guts would be spilling from split skin, trusty lungs floating off like balloons from a kids' party. The steady pressure creates the boundaries of my existence; I can live it out within those strong seams.

And yes, there *is* a freedom in taking it off at the end of the day, inhabiting the body simply as it is. Taking deep, full breaths. I can force a dissociated ambivalence towards my body, if I am alone and distracted. But only then.

Sometimes I buy fruit and watch it rot. I begin with the best of intentions, a determined thing akin to hope swelling gently inside me like bread trying to rise without enough yeast. I buy groceries for the first time in a month or longer – shame, for once, overpowering lethargic apathy – and rest a bunch of bananas on the kitchen windowsill, or a bag of grapes on the lowest shelf in the fridge.

In the first few days I will eat roughly a third of what I have bought, forcing it down as the texture bothers me more with each bite. The sensory discomfort always becomes too much; I finally, inevitably, give up.

It lasts weeks. I watch as brown creeps through banana skin, turning it spotted and rancid, eventually leaving nothing but mush. I watch as grapes grow soggy and wrinkled, collapsing in on themselves in a sticky soup. It is a discomfiting glimpse into the reality of this universe. Entropy, in the everyday.

There's a certain pleasure in paranoia. Losing yourself in the melodrama of it all. I once lived a long period of feeling very little, so I like to overdo things – emotions, gestures, words, thoughts. I like to overthink especially. There is nothing so darkly comforting as latching onto a single bad feeling, and then another, and another, and weaving them into a closed circuit of self-pity in which to wallow. Add a dash of songs that treat pain as a sacred thing, and you have the recipe for a soothing melancholia, as easy to slip into as a warm bed on a winter morning.

It's often preferable to the alternative. Despite my frustration with the stereotype of the disturbed genius, only able to create while truly in the depths of despair, any positive state that lasts longer than 48 hours tends to make me despair of losing my 'spark'. Sometimes when I'm happy, I worry that I'll be happy forever, and I'll never have anything to write about again – or perhaps I'll lose the ability to write altogether. What a foolish thing to fear. Every upswing meets its end, usually a sudden and jarring one. Happiness is fragile; depression is a renewable resource.

I go for a massage, my first in years probably. My back is knotted tight, a wind-up toy that broke before it could trigger the release. As if to compensate for the fact that the massage therapist will see me unbound and vulnerable, I rasp out the deepest voice I can muster. The words sound jagged, scraped raw like a child's knee after stacking it on a bike. She asks for a name; I give one that is unquestionably male. A signpost. I spend half my life dropping hints, and the other half watching them go unnoticed, a breadcrumb trail that few think to follow.

It hurts. My back is a lost cause, a write-off – the product of a sedentary lifestyle punctuated by full days of binding and tram trips that require a contortionist's skillset to make it out unscathed. Each time she pushes in on the muscle and waits for it to give way, there is a moment that I think it never will. That her hand will be there forever, pushing against my stubborn body like Sisyphus with his boulder.

It hurts, but I'll take pain over discomfort any day. It's the best kind of pain – the kind that has a reason for its infliction, the kind that breaks you down to your lowest common denominator and pieces you back together again. Surrendering the care of the body to another. Touch with a purpose.

My therapist thinks I have a deep discomfort with being alone with my thoughts, and that this is why I despise silence. Why I fill every moment with music or Netflix or conversation or the recently rediscovered strangeness of daytime television. I don't see why anyone should want to be alone with their thoughts in the first place. The closest I come to that is writing, and even then I cling to some kind of background noise. I write in little snatches of time, riding the bursts of inspiration until they've dissipated and I have to reach for an antidote to the deafening vacuum of silence.

I sleep on a mattress in the centre of my new living room, listening to the passing of cars – it sounds like the ocean. There are boxes lined up against corners, along walls, but still there is more unfilled space than I know what to do with. The only furniture: a TV, a few small cabinets, and a teal couch, low to the ground, that looks lonely and a little out of place. It feels very bare. It feels far too freeing. My bed has been set up for days, but I can't yet bring myself to move from this room, an open space with high ceilings and large windows.

I don't like choices and I don't like change. A routine has been established, something comforting and familiar, and I will stick to it until I am forced to do otherwise.

I listen to my artificial ocean, bask in the echoes of neon glows from the shops below. I wake up soaked in sun. I feel small, under that soaring ceiling. Small and safe.

bio next page >

Maddox Gifford is a writer and editor, a student of RMIT's Professional Writing and Editing program, and an activist first and foremost. Maddox grew up on Worimi and Awabakal lands, and now lives and studies on Wurundjeri land. Maddox enjoys reading, passionate discussions, writing – once it's over – and depression naps.